YORK NOT

General Editors: Professo
of Stirling) & Professor Su
University of Beirut)

Alan Bennett

TALKING HEADS

Notes by Delia Dick

BA (OPEN UNIVERSITY) MA (WARWICK)

Lecturer in twentieth-century literature,
Universities of Warwick and Coventry

LONGMAN
YORK PRESS

YORK PRESS
Immeuble Esseily, Place Riad Solh, Beirut

ADDISON WESLEY LONGMAN LIMITED
Edinburgh Gate, Harlow,
Essex CM20 2JE, United Kingdom
Associated companies, branches and representatives
throughout the world

First published 1996
Third impression 1997

ISBN 0–582–29349 9

Phototypeset by Gem Graphics, Trenance, Mawgan Porth, Cornwall
Printed in Singapore

Contents

Part 1

Introduction

The life and works of Alan Bennett

Alan Bennett was born in 1934 in Leeds, in the county of Yorkshire, where he also grew up and was educated. He was the second of two sons, and his father worked as a butcher for the local Co-operative Society stores. When he was five years old, the Second World War broke out, and his whole childhood and early teenage years were, like those of most of his contemporaries, spent living through austere, disciplined times, with food and clothing rationed. He attended the local Upper Armley National School, followed by Leeds Modern School. By his own account he was a shy, bookish child, and fervently religious in his teens. When he left school it was with the offer of a place at Sydney Sussex College, Cambridge. However, two years' compulsory National Service intervened and he was sent on the Joint Services Language Course to learn Russian at Bodmin in Cornwall and later at Cambridge. Having enjoyed a taste of university life there, he decided to try for Oxford, and succeeded in gaining an Open Scholarship in history at Exeter College.

Alan Bennett was a teenager in the 1950s and a young man in the 1960s – decades that witnessed dramatic changes in the structure of society. Until then, especially in the provinces where lifestyles changed only slowly, the Church was held in high esteem and the clergy in a local community were genuinely respected figures. Equally respected were the elderly and, as there was relatively little social mobility, families – particularly working-class ones – were more closely knit, the elderly were not expected to live in isolation, and neighbours were far more knowledgeable about each other's lives and in most cases more supportive. Girls were expected to marry, and were brought up to think that sex before marriage was wrong (that is not to say that it did not take place, but it was certainly secretive). It was a hierarchical society with a firm (many would call it rigid) structure. The 1960s, with its explosion of free love, anarchic values and focus on youth, changed all that for good, and the feeling of release from stifling traditional constraints made it an exciting time to live through.

Too self-conscious as a student to join OUDS (the Oxford University Dramatic Society) or the Experimental Theatre Club, Alan Bennett nevertheless found his way to dramatic success through the end-of-term junior common room smoking concerts. These were, he writes, 'uproarious drunken affairs . . . in the direct line of those camp concerts POWs [Prisoners of War] spent their time in acting when they weren't busy tunnelling under the foundations' (*Writing Home*, p. 18). For one of these concerts Alan Bennett wrote a parody of an Anglican vicar's sermon, a form with which he was very familiar.

This 'sermon' (now said to be on the syllabus of several theological courses) was very well received at the Edinburgh Festival Fringe and the various reviews in fact earned Alan Bennett a place in the satirical revue *Beyond the Fringe*, the following year. He was invited along with Dudley Moore, also from Oxford, and Jonathan Miller and Peter Cook from Cambridge, to put together the original version of *Beyond the Fringe* as an official Edinburgh Festival revue in 1960. *Beyond the Fringe* enjoyed a run in London's West End the following year, and went on Broadway in New York in 1962.

By this time Alan Bennett was a postgraduate at Oxford, working as a temporary tutor in history at Exeter College and Magdalen College. He did not enjoy teaching, finding is so difficult to produce enough discussion points to fill the tuition hours, he claims, that he resorted to putting the clock forward before sessions. He hoped that 'the celebrity of the revue to some degree compensated my pupils for the shortcomings of the tuition' (*Writing Home*, p. 21).

Since his brilliant success in *Beyond the Fringe*, which was a turning point in his career, Alan Bennett has often acted and sometimes directed, but his primary occupation has been writing for the stage and television. He has written over twenty plays, his stage plays including the satirical comedies *Forty Years On* (produced in 1968), *Getting On* (1971) and *Habeas Corpus* (1973). *The Old Country* (1977), a darker work, is concerned with the life of an English spy in what used to be the Soviet Union and his decision whether or not to return to an England that has radically changed. His most recent stage successes have been a new version of *The Wind in the Willows*, performed at the Royal National Theatre in 1990, and *The Madness of George III*, first performed at the same theatre in 1991, and later made into a film. His published work for television consists of groups of plays, published under the titles *Objects of Affection and Other Plays for Television*, *The Writer in Disguise*, *Two Kafka Plays*, *Talking Heads* and *Single Spies*.

In 1994 he published *Writing Home*, a collection of talks, diaries and occasional journalism, which contains much revealing information about his life and the sources of his material.

'Speaking properly' and 'Being yourself'

Alan Bennett sees a division in his view of the world, brought about by growing up in the provinces and living his adult life mainly in London. He is conscious of 'an anxiety about sincerity' in the way he writes. He illustrates what he thinks is a split in his literary integrity by what, in *Writing Home*, he describes as the 'parable' of his mother's chance meeting with T. S. Eliot. In his work as a butcher Alan Bennett's father's customers included a Mrs Fletcher, whose daughter Valerie became the second wife of the poet. One day Mrs Bennett met Mrs Fletcher in the street with her son-in-law, and introductions were made. Mrs Bennett had met and spoken to the great poet T. S. Eliot, although at the same time she was completely unaware of his literary significance. Alan Bennett explains that for him this meeting encompassed an image of how, when he began to write, it was in 'two different voices', a metropolitan voice – 'speaking properly' – and a provincial voice – 'being yourself'. T. S. Eliot represented Art, Culture and Literature, written with capital letters and to do with 'speaking properly', and his mother represented life, 'resolutely', as he says, 'in the lower case', and concerned with 'being yourself'.

In his first works, his sketches for revues and his stage plays, Alan Bennett wrote with what he claims was an assumed voice, the voice that he had met in novels or at Saturday matinées at the local theatre – 'metropolitan, literary and middle-class'. His first attempt at 'being himself' and using his 'Northern voice' was, he writes, a complete failure. In a refurbished version of *Beyond the Fringe* on Broadway in 1963, one of his new sketches was a humorous monologue about death, as it might be viewed in the North of England. This was a topic that was somewhat taboo at that time, especially as a subject of humour, and the setting of the North of England was almost guaranteed to be incomprehensible to a New York audience.

Alan Bennett says that 'It's in the process of imitating the voices of others that one comes to learn the sound of one's own'. He feels that the dichotomy between metropolitan and provincial still persists. He has found that for him, as a general rule, his personal voice, the voice he was born with, has been most suited to his television plays. In any case, he has come to the conclusion that, for a writer these days, having two voices is 'more a worry about consistency' than a serious problem.

In *Talking Heads* Alan Bennett is often 'being himself' and, as he puts it, using the voice with which he was born. And it is clear that much of his material has been plundered from his past. He claims, like the poet Philip Larkin (1922–85), that his childhood was 'unspent' in a provincial city, and that life which 'did not live up to literature' was something that happened elsewhere. His parents were diffident people, feeling that their lack of confidence was due to inadequate education. Alan Bennett does not concur with this view, insisting that even his extended education failed to make him a confident figure in the world. Wartime shortages and the failure of life to come up to the standard of children's stories with their expansive, middle-class, country backgrounds and frequent adventures left him with a sense of disappointment. The ordinariness of his childhood meant that he could claim neither to have been privileged nor deprived.

Nevertheless, if life in Leeds could not be lived on a grand scale of adventure or wretchedness, it proved a training ground for those skills which can be associated with Alan Bennett's short television plays, and particularly *Talking Heads*. 'Gossip as drama' is a phrase which has been used of his work as he has a keen ear for the nuances of trivial conversation. His dialogue retains total authenticity, whilst he re-works and heightens it for dramatic and usually tragi-comic purposes. Although the social level of his characters is often different, he has been described as the natural successor to Betjeman because of his memorable touch in writing about the familiar. Like Sir John Betjeman (1906–84; poet laureate, 1972), he captures the minutiae of everyday life over and over again, by references to details he has stored away, sometimes from his childhood days. For instance, Wilfred's ambition in *A Cream Cracker Under the Settee* to take up fretwork and make toys and money, is based on a memory of Alan Bennett's father and the toys he made for his sons in the Second World War. In *Bed Among the Lentils*, Susan's narrative brings in several quotations from the Book of Common Prayer, a work with which, Alan Bennett recalls in *Writing Home*, he was very familiar, having 'learned large sections by heart' as a devout Anglican when he was young. Like Susan, he became an agnostic but nevertheless still finds the language compelling. In the 'Introduction' to *Talking Heads* the author traces Susan's shaken belief to a timid grafitto in a school hymn book, which said 'Get lost, Jesus'.

Other sources of material are related to what Alan Bennett would call his 'metropolitan' aspect. He mentions that the funeral of Muriel Carpenter's husband in *Soldiering On* was suggested by that of a friend's father who, too, had 'touched life at many points'. Lesley, he claims in the 'Introduction', is based upon many unsuccessful small-part actors he has seen auditioned, whose estimation of the importance of their previous work bears little relation to fact. In *Writing Home* he describes how in New York in 1980 he was persuaded to attend a 'theatrical experience' which turned out to be an Alcoholics Anonymous meeting: 'My name is Barbara, I am an alcoholic . . .' and so on – obviously useful in *Bed Among the Lentils*.

Although an actor who can assume many personae, Alan Bennett, as himself, is a familiar figure by now on the television screen, and he has perhaps resolved his supposed problem of the division between his 'metropolitan' self and his 'provincial' self. As a guide around Westminster Abbey in a series of three television programmes over the Christmas period of 1995, he was certainly 'being himself'. His familiar Northern vowels – over which he claims to have spent much time in indecisive agonising – and his confident knowledge about the history of the Abbey seemed to be equally parts of the one person. His often amusing but always straight-faced commentary, with its occasionally melancholy overtones, was typical, too, of the writer or, at least, of his public face.

The intimacy of the television screen has offered opportunities in *Talking Heads* which Alan Bennett has been able to realise fully. The economy of the form may have appealed, as has been suggested, to the BBC in the financial difficulties of the Eighties, but it also demonstrated the author's ability to pull off a *tour de force* within constrained limits. The plays, too, demanded accomplished actors and those involved met the challenge. Students of these texts may well have to read them as short stories, if video or audio tapes are not readily accessible. The plays are sometimes performed on the stage and you may be lucky enough to see a production of one or more. Desirable as it is to see plays in performance, however, the texts of *Talking Heads* do stand very well by themselves: as Alan Bennett says in his 'Introduction', there is a 'single point of view' with a sole narrator in each play'; as he adds, the experience of watching a narrative told by one actor is more like reading a short story than watching a play. Since so much of the story involves people and events not seen by the viewer, an effort of imagination similar to that required in reading a story has to come into play.

A note on the text and television productions

The text is that of Alan Bennett, *Talking Heads*, BBC Books, 1988, and the video of the same name by BBC Television Productions, 1988. The video contains:

A Chip in the Sugar GRAHAM – Alan Bennett, directed by Stuart Burge
Bed Among the Lentils SUSAN – Maggie Smith, directed by Alan Bennett
A Lady of Letters IRENE RUDDOCK – Patricia Routledge, directed by Giles Foster
Her Big Chance LESLEY – Julie Walters, directed by Giles Foster
Soldiering On MURIEL – Stephanie Cole, directed by Tristram Powell
A Cream Cracker Under the Settee DORIS – Thora Hird, directed by Stuart Burge

Part 2

Summaries
of TALKING HEADS

A Chip in the Sugar

The play takes place in the sparsely furnished bedroom of the narrator, Graham Whittaker, 'a mild, middle-aged man'.

[Scene 1] Graham remembers how the previous day he and his seventy-two-year-old mother had been out in town when Mrs Whittaker had fallen on the pavement as Graham had been trying to disengage her arm from his. One of the helpful passers-by was Frank Turnbull, a long-lost friend of Mrs Whittaker from before her marriage – apparently an early admirer of whose existence Graham had been unaware. Frank, taking charge, led them to a café; this, unlike Graham's discreet favourite place, was decorated in red plastic and there was a careless chip in the sugar. Frank, a men's outfitter, criticised Graham's clothes and when he learned of Graham's long-term mental health problems was extremely unsympathetic.

[Scene 2] Some time later, in late afternoon: Graham describes the day's events. The vicar called for a donation to famine relief. Frank Turnbull then arrived and took Mrs Whittaker out in his car. Graham was not invited. He has been reading a magazine and fears that he is suffering from a recurrence of his anxiety symptoms, since he thinks he has heard someone knocking at the door – a delusion he has experienced in the past.

[Scene 3] Another day, at night: Mrs Whittaker and Frank have been to York. Graham's mother announced to him that she and Frank were planning to be married. The honeymoon would be in Tenerife. She tells Graham to take one of his 'tablets'. Graham would be expected to move out to a hostel where he had spent some previous time. Graham can't sleep and thinks someone is watching the house.

[Scene 4] Soon after the previous scene, in the evening: Graham has been to a self-help therapy group at the Health Centre that morning. They discussed Mrs Whittaker's prospective marriage, but Graham found the group's attitude unhelpful. Later in the day, when Mrs Whittaker and Frank Turnbull had gone out for holiday purchases, Graham became aware that there really was someone knocking at the door, and was relieved that it had not been a figment of his imagination and the return of a symptom of his illness. The caller was Frank Turnbull's daughter.

[Scene 5] A day or two later, at night: Graham tells us that when Mrs Whittaker returned he broke the news to her that Frank Turnbull was a philanderer with an invalid wife. His daughter, who looked after her mother, had been obliged – not for the first time – to warn an unsuspecting victim that she was being misled. Mrs Whittaker, finally persuaded of the truth and understandably upset, behaved spitefully to Graham, saying that he was not normal and revealing that she knew he kept a store of pornographic magazines in his bedroom. However, by the following morning she seemed to have recovered her equanimity and the play ends with Graham describing the resumption of their usual life together.

NOTES AND GLOSSARY:

vis-à-vis:	in relation to
spent a penny:	euphemism for went to the lavatory
diddling her hands:	dabbling her hands in the water
bifocals:	spectacles with lenses partly for near and partly for distant vision
she's wiring in:	she's eating enthusiastically
flares are anathema:	flared trousers are totally unacceptable
pulling your socks up:	making an effort
Featherbedding:	making things easy for someone
snotty:	snooty, snobbish
over the moon:	delighted
my whack:	my share
getting our skates on:	hurrying
spanking:	superb
he's your fancy man in embryo:	he's your prospective lover
the ghetto approach:	the segregated approach
Toodle pip:	goodbye
suited:	satisfied

Bed Among the Lentils

The narrator in the play is Susan, wife of an ambitious vicar, Geoffrey.

[Scene 1] On a Sunday evening before Easter, in the vicarage kitchen: Susan describes her day. She was late for communion and did not enjoy her husband's sermon on sex as an offering to God. The parish has learned that the bishop is to pay a visit. In the afternoon, avoiding Geoffrey's overtures, she said that she was delivering the parish magazine, but in fact spent the afternoon in the car in a lay-by. She discusses her lack of interest in her role of vicar's wife and reveals that in the evening she went to the local off-licence to buy more sherry.

[Scene 2] After Easter. Afternoon, in the side-chapel: The bishop's visit to the vicarage for lunch has not gone well. Susan has not responded satisfactorily to his enquiries about her commitment and she has spilled tinned milk on his gaiters. (This incident confirms what Susan has not actually admitted – that she is a heavy and usually secret drinker.) Later, Susan tells us, she went into Leeds to see a handsome Asian shopkeeper, Ramesh Ramesh, whom she has discovered as a discreet source of alcohol. They sit in the back of his shop and talk about themselves and about Hinduism.

[Scene 3] Some time later. Morning, in the vicarage kitchen: After describing how her life is not turning out as she would have wished, Susan gives an amusing account of an attempt at flower arranging with Mrs Shrubsole, Mrs Belcher and Miss Frobisher in the church. This ended in an accident when she fell, drunkenly attempting to demonstrate the short-comings of an elaborate arrangement made by one of the parishioners. She was taken back to the vicarage to lie down while the ladies made a fuss of Geoffrey and generally humiliated her. Later in the day she went to Leeds and, to her surprise, found herself making love with Ramesh, who had closed his shop early.

[Scene 4] Summer. Afternoon, in the vestry: Susan has drunk the communion wine and Geoffrey was unable to begin the service on the second Sunday after Trinity. Susan claims that she thought she had solved the problem by suggesting that he substitute cough mixture. Geoffrey was angry, but in fact used it and no one noticed the difference. She describes how she missed Evensong and went to see Ramesh, whose love-making among the lentil sacks was a revelation to her.

[Scene 5] Months later, in the vicarage drawing room: Susan, looking unusually smart, describes how Ramesh persuaded her to give up drinking, although Geoffrey has taken the credit for it. His public pronouncements about the problems he believes they have come through together, as a triumph for his supposed support and understanding, helped to promote his career plans. Susan's narrative ends with Geoffrey in line for a senior clerical appointment and Ramesh having moved to Preston after fetching his young wife from India. Though apparently a reformed character, Susan is as unconvinced as ever about the value of her role as a clergyman's wife – and she now has what she sees as the additional burden of regular attendance at tedious meetings of Alcoholics Anonymous.

NOTES AND GLOSSARY:

the Garden of Gethsemane: the scene of the agony of Jesus Christ on the Mount of Olives, before he gives himself up for crucifixion

Almighty God, unto whom . . .: Collect, a short prayer from the Anglican communion service

bring home the bacon: support the household financially, be the bread-winner

off licence: a shop selling alcoholic drink for consumption else-where

Meals on Wheels: a voluntary organisation taking hot meals to the elderly and disabled daily

Carnation milk: milk from a tin, as are the peaches. Like the 'flabby lasagne', they imply that Susan has not gone to much effort to prepare the meal in honour of the bishop's visit

Mary Magdalen and the Nivea cream: reference to Mary Magdalen and her anointing of Jesus's feet with expensive oils (although Nivea cream is an inexpensive emollient cosmetic product)

instant: instant coffee

getting up to all sorts: the gods and goddesses are in various erotic postures

WI: Women's Institute – a rural organisation for craftwork and social activities, established in Britain in 1915

vestry: church robing room

Gert and Daisy: a well-known music hall double act earlier in the 20th century, performed by Elsie and Doris Waters

The Wind in the Willows: children's story by Kenneth Grahame (1859–1932) with animal characters and set in woodland and on the river bank (dramatised for the National Theatre by Alan Bennett)

Bambi: film by Walt Disney about a fawn

HAZFLOR: a parody of the HAZCHEM sign indicating dangerous chemicals

Duraglit: Duraglit is a brass polishing product.

Emily Brontë: English novelist (1818–48), author of *Wuthering Heights* who died tragically of TB at an early age

lighten our darkness . . . : Third Collect of Anglican evening prayer

wanny: feeble

AA: Alcoholics Anonymous

rural dean: the head of a section of country clergy

the road to Damascus: St Paul experienced a vision of Jesus on his way to Damascus – this determined the future course of his life

young upwardly mobile parsons: pun on young, upwardly mobile persons, or YUPPIES, a feature of 1980s life

A Lady of Letters

The narrator in this play is Miss Irene Ruddock, an 'ordinary middle-aged woman' who lives alone.

[Scene 1] Afternoon, in a bay-windowed room: Miss Ruddock describes the funeral service (for Miss Pringle, a casual acquaintance) that she has recently attended. We soon learn that she takes it upon herself to write letters of complaint on the slightest pretext. She has written to the director of the local crematorium about hearse drivers smoking outside the chapel, and is pleased that this has resulted in a brief correspondence. New neighbours have moved in opposite her house – a young couple with a child who, in Miss Ruddock's view, looks grubby.

[Scene 2] Some time later. Morning, in the same room: Miss Ruddock tells us more about a whole range of letters she has written, which have brought gratifying results. Her fountain pen is a prized present from her late, much loved mother. She has noticed a bruise on the arm of the child opposite and has heard it crying.

[Scene 3] A week or two have passed. It is afternoon: Miss Ruddock says that life in prison is too easy and leads to more crime. She writes regularly to her MP about crime, most recently about the undesirability of deploying constables who wear spectacles. She has just written to a sausage manufacturer about a hair she has found in their product that morning. Miss Ruddock is confirmed in her poor opinion of the young couple opposite: they are always out at night and no baby-sitter arrives.

[Scene 4] Dusk, on a different day. Miss Ruddock is at the window: Miss Ruddock tells us that her mother knew everyone in the street and regrets the loss of community spirit – a loss to which she does not realise she is contributing by her failure to communicate directly with those around her. Worried about the child opposite, she has been to the doctor – as usual, an unfamiliar figure to her in the large group practice – to tell him about her anxiety. We learn that she has problems with mental health – she 'gets upset' – and the doctor, referring to her medical notes, dismisses her fears as he writes out a new prescription.

[Scene 5] Some time later. A bare background: Miss Ruddock continues her narrative, apparently at the police station. The doctor, she tells us, had asked the vicar to call upon her but she cut short his evangelical attempts by telling him she was an atheist. Then she reveals that the police have called about anonymous letters she had been writing concerning the couple opposite, and we learn that Miss Ruddock has not previously been telling the whole truth about her apparently harmless letter writing. She has already been bound over to keep the peace by a magistrates' court after accusing the chemist's wife of being a prostitute and the crossing warden of being a child molester. The child opposite had not been neglected but had been ill with leukaemia, from which it had just died in hospital, and the police arrived to arrest her.

[Scene 6] A week or more later. Daytime, at home: Miss Ruddock tells us she has been given a suspended sentence for her malicious letter writing and now has two social workers, whom she does not appreciate, to help her. One of them insists on calling her Irene, much to her annoyance. They make various suggestions, none of which Miss Ruddock finds useful. She is now worried about a local police constable who is, she claims, spending a lot of time with a housewife further down the road.

[Scene 7] Some while afterwards. An institutional setting: Miss Ruddock has encountered a dramatic change, which brings about an unexpectedly buoyant ending to the play. She is in prison, having written one letter too many. But, surprisingly, she is having a wonderful time. Wearing an unfamiliar tracksuit and happy to be 'Irene' to all the other inmates, she is thoroughly enjoying the prison classes and even looking forward to a job when she is released. She finds she has many skills, not least a most neglected one – the ability to lend a friendly ear to others' troubles. Some inmates have experienced harrowing circumstances in their lives and Miss Ruddock weighs their difficulties against her own – 'You don't know you're born, I think.' Unlikely though it may be to find fulfilment in prison, Miss Ruddock acknowledges her happiness.

NOTES AND GLOSSARY:

tab-ends:	cigarette ends
Platignum:	the brand name of Miss Ruddock's fountain pen
Awayday:	one-day reduced-price railway ticket
Basildon Bond:	a brand of writing paper
shantung:	natural silk
SS:	(*German*) Schutz-Staffel – Nazi special police force, notorious for their brutality

---

Her Big Chance

The story is told by Lesley, an actress in her early thirties.

[Scene 1] Morning, Lesley's flat: Lesley has recently finished making a film, she tells us. She describes a walk-on part she once played in a TV serial, explains her dedication to her work and how she prides herself on being a professional. It is already obvious that Lesley is a silly, self-deluding woman, whose estimation of her gifts we are not likely to accept. Going back to the film and the means by which she was given the role, she describes how at a party she met Spud, a man who said he was 'on the production side' of film work. He arranged an audition for Lesley the next morning and offered her a bed nearby for the night. In spite of her slick protestations, it is clear that Lesley expected to have to sleep with Spud in exchange for his help. She was disappointed when she assessed from his vest and his tattoo that he was an electrician. She is well-versed in these matters.

[Scene 2] A few weeks earlier, after the audition. Afternoon, Lesley's flat: Lesley is very pleased with her performance at the audition, which was for the role of a character called Travis. The first requirement was for Lesley to strip to her underclothes, since in the film Travis spends most of her time sunbathing on board a yacht. Lesley was quite happy to undress, and this part of the audition was successful. Lesley then re-enacts the discussion which followed, with her attempts at bright conversation and all the suggestions she made for developing the character of Travis. Simon, who interviewed her, said that they needed someone who could water-ski and perhaps play chess, and we guess that he was astonished by Lesley's pretentiousness. Lesley ends the scene surprised that she has heard no more.

[Scene 3] A week or so later. Morning, a dismal dressing-room on the film set at Lee-on-Solent: Lesley tells us that, at the last minute, she was telephoned by Nigel, the director's assistant, and offered the part of Travis. So far she has not been on the set. It appears that Nigel thought that she could water-ski – he has contacted the wrong girl, we suspect – and this is essential to the script. A local girl has been doubling for her. The make-up and wardrobe man, Scott, was disagreeable to her from the first, but the evening before she met Terry, a cameraman. They went out for the evening and later Lesley shared his room, which she says was nicer than hers.

[Scene 4] Later, during filming. Evening, Lesley's hotel room: Lesley describes a day's filming which she spent pretending to sunbathe on the deck of the yacht, whilst the actors playing her elderly lover and his business associate were the focal point. When she describes how Nigel persuaded her to take off first her bikini top and then the bottom, it becomes clear to us that her role is to be limited to providing nude scenes. Nevertheless, Lesley persisted with her ideas for building up Travis's film personality and was humoured a little by Nigel and the director, Gunther, in exchange, we guess, for her compliancy. In the evening Lesley discovered that everyone had gone out again (without her) to supper at the restaurant run by her water-skiing stand-in. Eventually in the bar she met Kenny, the animal handler on the film. She went to his room to see the animals and stayed the night.

[Scene 5] After the end of filming. Dusk, Lesley's flat: Lesley describes the climax of the film, when she was required to kill her lover with a harpoon gun. She lost what was to have been her 'big line', about having a headache, which she explains to her own satisfaction. She has been making suggestions which she believes will assist the director to the end. On the last night she went to bed with Gunther and learned that the film would come out on video in Germany and perhaps Turkey; unlike Lesley, we have already understood that she has had a small role in a low grade crime film involving violence and nudity. Lesley ends this scene by describing her plans to take up various random interests and further develop her personality.

NOTES AND GLOSSARY:

Crossroads:	television serial, 1964–88, set in a motel
are you on cans:	are you in contact with the director – through your earphones

Woman in a Musquash Coat: identification of an 'extra' in the filming
Richard Attenborough: British film actor

Tess:	film version of the novel *Tess of the D'Urbervilles*, by Thomas Hardy (1840–1928)
Ciao:	(*Italian*) Goodbye
p.o.v.:	point of view
knockers:	(*slang*) breasts
a hair in the gate:	fault in the film caused by a blemish on the lens
West Germany:	between 1949 and 1990 Germany was divided in two, the larger part being known as 'West Germany'

Soldiering On

The narrator is Muriel Carpenter, a conventionally dressed middle-class woman in her late fifties.

[Scene 1] The day after her husband's funeral. Afternoon, a room in Muriel's comfortable house: Muriel's husband, Ralph, has died and she recounts the events of the previous day, when the funeral took place. We can see that, in spite of her emotional state, she had put the needs of her guests first. The range of Ralph's connections was wide: mourners were present who knew him through work, the army, the Church, sport and various charities. We learn that Muriel's son, Giles, and his wife and children were a great help. Her daughter, Margaret, had kept out of the way but appeared when the mourners had left. She did not seem to understand about her father's death and Muriel gave her a tablet to calm her.

[Scene 2] Some days later. Evening, Muriel is in an armchair: Muriel tells us about disposing of her husband's personal possessions. Following what she knew was Ralph's approach to any new situation, she tried to find out what help and advice was available to the newly bereaved. There was little, but everyone told her not to take any big decisions. In spite of this, she allowed Giles to persuade her, after a lavish lunch out, to let him invest money on her behalf. Ralph had left her very well off. Giles also took away some valuable items to hide in order to circumvent tax assessment (probate). Margaret, we learn, has suffered from the delusion that the police were coming to take her away. Muriel and Mabel, her trusted housekeeper or home help, had a struggle to get Margaret upstairs to bed and administer a tablet. We learn that Muriel's daughter has had long-term mental health problems.

[Scene 3] Some days or weeks later. Afternoon: Muriel has been writing letters. Margaret has had to go into hospital. Previously she has been looked after under what Muriel considers ideal conditions in a private nursing home. Now Muriel is upset that, because Giles has told her she cannot afford it, Margaret is in an overcrowded National Health psychiatric hospital where the facilities are very poor. Muriel is writing letters to her many contacts to try to raise money for mental health resources. Mental illness is a mystery, she says. Giles has told her, puzzlingly, that there is no capital available for her to start a small business.

[Scene 4] Some weeks later. Afternoon, Muriel is in a bare room: Giles's investment plans have turned out disastrously: many people have been financially ruined, including Muriel, although Giles's own property is secure. We can see that his mother still does not recognise that Giles is a scoundrel. Muriel's house and contents have had to be sold by auction, but she tells us that she finds she does not really care very much for possessions. Margaret's psychiatrist has told Muriel that he believes his patient is improving and has asked how she and her father got on together when she was a child.

[Scene 5] A month or more later. Evening, Muriel is in a boarding-house room in Hunstanton: Muriel has been swimming. She is now living on her own and it is clear that she has very little money, even for food. She tells us how she has tried to become part of the local community by offering to use her organising skills to help with local Meals On Wheels. At the local town hall they think she is asking for help, not offering it, and she realises she is considered too old. Margaret is much better, hoping to be able to live independently in her own flat. Giles has not been able to touch the money her father left her. Muriel has finally understood that Ralph abused his daughter and she and Margaret have been able to talk about this without acrimony. Giles and his family have cut themselves off. Muriel has become dependent on television and a personal stereo. She remains, as ever, undefeated by circumstances.

NOTES AND GLOSSARY:

beef en croute: beef cooked in pastry

the old Colchester days: Colchester is an army base, which suggests that Ralph has been a professional soldier

Massey-Ferguson: a tractor-making firm for which Ralph presumably worked

light the blue touch paper and retire: light the firework and stand back – here, introduce two people and hope they will get on together

Household Brigade: a brigade from the élite troops who normally guard the sovereign

chocker: (*slang*) full – probably from 'chock-a-block'

blub: (*slang*) weep – from 'blubber'

gone into floods: gone into floods of tears

Hawes and Curtis: tailors of Jermyn Street, London SW1

a little zizz: a little sleep, nap

liquidity problem: lack of readily accessible funds

'... the index is going down': quoted share prices on the Stock Market are falling

the revenue: tax officials

Meals On Wheels: a public service whereby meals are delivered (by volunteers who give their service free) to the homes of the elderly or disabled

'... drag our brogues ...': usually 'drag our feet' – postpone doing something

Siena: medieval city in Tuscany, Italy

Napoleonic Wars: series of French campaigns, under Napoleon I, against Britain and other European powers from 1800 to 1815

Nikolaus Pevsner: 1902–83 – well-known writer on art and architecture

qua **building, not displeasing:** as a building, attractive enough architecturally

National Trust: trust for the preservation of places of historic interest or national beauty, founded 1895

different ball game: US cliché for a marked change from something familiar

NUPE: National Union of Public Employees

A propos: on the subject (of)

'All hands to the pumps': everyone needs to respond to the emergency

nouvelle: nouvelle cuisine – an elaborate cooking style of the 1980s, offering very small portions

Lay not up for yourself treasures on earth: see the Bible, Matthew 6:19

The lilies of the field: see the Bible, Matthew 6:28

Sloane Street: fashionable address of Giles's home in London

cossy: (*slang, originally Australian*) swimming costume

The Lady: monthly magazine catering for conventional middle-class women

2 i/c: second in command

orphans of the storm: traditional reference to a desperate situation, perhaps referring to a once-familiar painting or melodrama

young man in orange: follower of so-called 'Hare Krishna' cult

precinct: here, shopping area

prep: preparation

Peter Pan: statue in Kensington Gardens, London, of a character, the perpetually young Peter Pan, in Sir James Barrie's

(1860–1937) play for children of that name, first
produced in 1904

Science Museum: in Kensington, London

A Cream Cracker Under the Settee

The narrator is Doris, a frail woman of seventy-five.

[Scene 1] Morning, the living room of Doris's semi-detached house. Doris is sitting on a low chair: Doris has fallen and hurt her leg, she tells us, as she tries to rub the numbness away. Her home help, Zulema, who has just finished her weekly visit, has told her that she must not attempt housework, but Doris is unimpressed by Zulema's cleaning and she fell after clambering onto a stool in order to dust the top of a framed wedding photograph of herself and her late husband, Wilfred. She is not in good health, we gather, since she is forbidden housework, suffers from dizzy spells and has a pacemaker; her worst fear is that she will have to go into a local old people's home, Stafford House. She worries about the gate banging and about leaves from next door on the path of her front garden. Her leg is still numb but she decides to try to get up to make a cup of tea.

[Scene 2] Later that day, the living room. Doris is sitting on the floor, leaning against the wall: It is apparent that Doris's leg gave way when she tried to get up and she is now on the floor, from which vantage point she sees 'a cream cracker under the settee', evidence of Zulema's superficial cleaning. We learn more about Doris's obsession with cleanliness and hygiene, as she describes hobbies she has apparently discouraged Wilfred from taking up in the past, fearing mess and 'muck'. She would, however, have allowed him a small dog, in spite of 'all the little hairs' but Wilfred, we guess, was unlikely to have been able to persist in the face of his wife's disapproval. When someone comes through the gate, she thinks help might be coming, but it turns out to be only a child who urinates in her front garden, to Doris's disgust. She decides to try to get to the front door which she might be able to open to get help.

[Scene 3] Later, in the hall. Doris is now on the floor with her back to the front door: Doris is reminded of the big pram which had stood in the hall, and which Wilfred had bought when she was pregnant in the early days of their marriage. She cannot reach the lock to open the door and is dozing when a leaflet is pushed through the letter-box. Her calls for help are not heard by the leaflet deliverer. We learn that her one child was apparently stillborn. The midwife wrapped him up in newspaper, Doris remembers resentfully. She thinks how different life might be now if she had had children and grandchildren. Her other leg begins to feel numb, too.

[Scene 4] Evening, the living room. Doris is propped up against the sofa: She talks about clothes she has had made for her and all the baby's things she has put away upstairs. She eats the cream cracker from under the sofa. Her mind wanders to Zulema and the threat of a move to Stafford House – now, she realises, imminent. We learn how she would loathe to go there because she thinks that all the 'old lasses' would smell of urine and she would have to 'mix' – something she and Wilfred did not do. She contrasts her image of Stafford House with a happy memory of early married life, when Wilfred and she would have their 'tea' together and she was expecting a baby. Everyone was clean, she remembers, and all the neighbours were friendly. By the time the local policeman knocks at the door to ask if she is all right, it seems she has decided that, rather than go to Stafford House, she will let nature take its course. She calls out to the policeman, pretending all is well. She speaks as though to Wilfred and then voices her final thoughts, which go back to her memory of an idyllic childhood bedtime, when she was washed and in a clean nightdress, ready to be tucked up for the night.

NOTES AND GLOSSARY:

Ewbank: brand name of a carpet sweeper
Pull your horns in: be less ambitious
buffet: (*dialect*) stool
sneck: (*dialect*) catch, gate fastening
en route: on the way
them frame things: walking supports
jump the gun: act prematurely
costume: suit
side the pots: clear the table
My Alice Blue Gown: popular song of the early twentieth century

Part 3

Commentary

The title

talking head: a person appearing on television who merely talks, either directly to the audience, or in discussion with others in the studio, rather than presenting information in a more visually entertaining manner. Used in the world of the media since the late 1970s

(*The Shorter Slang Dictionary*, Routledge, 1994)

It would seem from the definition above that a 'talking head' is a synonym for boredom in a television age of dazzling – sometimes bewildering – visual entertainment. This is a challenge that Alan Bennett confronts in more ways than one.

First, he capitalises on the intimacy that the television screen can offer to drama; the long camera 'takes' draw us into the narrator's world in a way that the rapid change of angle and scene familiar in much of what is presented on television cannot. Our concentration is steadily invited, rather than fought for by multi-angled images. (Incidentally, it has been suggested that the economy of means of these monologues, so effective dramatically, was also well-suited to the economic constraints of the BBC's drama budget in the late '80s.)

Secondly, his characters' narratives are riveting rather than boring, because, just as he has been said to have made 'gossip into drama', so he has made an art-form out of the tedious. Recognisable as firmly based in real life as the dialogues are, they are nothing like verbatim transcripts of conversations, but are artfully contrived to convey the humour and the pathos of his characters' situations. Alan Bennett wrote another similar short play which preceded *Talking Heads*, called *A Woman of No Importance*, in which the actress who played Miss Ruddock played a Miss Schofield. He wrote of that narrator that '. . . to have her in full close-up, retailing in unremitting detail how, for instance, she borrowed the salt in the canteen, takes one beyond, I hope, tedium'. He thought that the more one knew about his characters, the more they could be understood. They each somehow justify a demand for our attention to their situation in a world which is not right for them.

The characters

GRAHAM in *A Chip in the Sugar*

We learn gradually from the narrator, Graham, that he has long-term problems of mental health and has to take 'tablets', especially at times of stress. He has lived in a hostel and has worked intermittently at therapeutic crafts such as flower- and soft-toy-making. But for a long time he has lived at home with his mother, taking charge of household chores and, although as Alan Bennett says in his 'Introduction', Graham 'would not accept that he is married to his mother', their relationship does have an established domestic quality about it. Mrs Whittaker is pleased when she is taken for Graham's wife by someone in the street; she skittishly refers to him later as her 'boyfriend' and likes to walk arm in arm with him. Although the realisation that he could even for a moment be taken for his mother's husband disturbs Graham, their interdependence seems to go deep: they enjoy little outings and Graham teaches his mother the liberal views which he has acquired from *The Guardian* newspaper. Like her son, she appreciates the niceties of different architectural styles and the 'classy' little cafes that he selects for their minor indulgences at tea and coffee times. So Graham is greatly disturbed that his mother should be easily won away from him by an admirer from a past so distant that it is even 'pre-Dad'. Her admirer, Frank Turnbull, is a vulgar little man, flashily dressed and with the views of the more reactionary tabloid newspapers. Graham is particularly wounded that his mother so readily rejects his ideas and becomes a mouthpiece for Frank.

The philistine and illiberal Frank has no sympathy for Graham's illness, saying that he thinks '... the solution to mental illness is hard physical work'. Graham becomes increasingly upset by his mother's defection and what seems like her collusion with a man who despises her son.

Soon there is a wedding in the offing and the expulsion of Graham from his mother's home is to follow – 'You were happy in the hostel. You rubbed shoulders with all sorts.' But the late-flowering romance ends with an explanation – off stage – from Frank's daughter. She is someone who, Graham believes, has been watching the house and who his mother thinks is a figment of his imagination, or a symptom of his illness. Frank is an aged Don Juan, it appears, who has taken advantage of other women before and is married to an invalid wife. Mrs Whittaker is upset, but recovers her dignity as domestic harmony is, more or less, restored.

'Harmony' is perhaps not quite the right word, since the relationship between Graham and Mrs Whittaker involves them in a constant low-level struggle for power, the object of which is to avoid allowing either to 'get it over' the other (i.e. take up a superior position). The account opens with an early morning conversation the day after Mrs Whittaker's (perhaps symbolic) fall and flirtatious encounter with Frank. Mrs Whittaker reassures Graham: 'I think the world of you.' He recipro- cates and during the reconciliations she challenges his tea-making skills: 'This tea looks strong' – but Graham reasserts his authority with: 'Give me your teeth, I'll swill them.' This undercurrent develops throughout the narrative, with Graham commenting, not always to his mother, on those faults and physical failings which he knows make her dependent upon him: her vanity, her poor memory, her 'unpredictable bowels'. Mrs Whittaker, who exhibits an almost adolescent fecklessness in her unex- pected fling with Frank, abandons all the values she supposedly shares with Graham and adopts Frank's views and style wholesale. Just as easily she reassumes Graham's interests at the end of the play: '. . . We like old buildings, don't we, you and me?' she says, as if nothing had happened, when they prepare for one of their familiar outings.

Although Mrs Whittaker is contrite and obviously prepared to make the best of her life with Graham again, her attempt at escape shows perhaps how trapped she had felt in her life with her son. Her lack of control on the previous night, when Graham had told her about Frank's perfidy, reveals cruelly to Graham how she thinks about him: 'How can you understand, you, you're not normal?' And, finally, she re-establishes her position, supposing that he might feel that his judgment over Frank had been superior to hers, shouting: 'You think you've got it over me, Graham Whittaker. Well, you haven't, I've got it over you . . . I know the kind of magazines you read.' 'Chess . . .' 'They never are chess. Chess with no clothes on. Chess in their birthday suits. That kind of chess. Chessmen.' He can only counter, reminding her of her weak memory: 'Go to bed. And turn your blanket off.' The play ends with much the same kind of balance of power with which it opened.

Mrs Whittaker, still lively, wins sympathy, although we never see her, and we understand how she is attracted to the vulgar but optimistic and 'natty' Frank: he is such a contrast to the timid Graham, far from 'natty' with his clammy feet, plastic mac and flared trousers, and with his constant pessimistic reminders of her growing frailties. Graham explains at the beginning of the monologue that his mother is not actually disabled, although she likes the added comfort of 'disabled' facilities in the public lavatories, but that 'her memory's bad'. Graham often has to tell her how old she is, for instance, and by the following day she has forgotten her fall in the street, although it has made her side feel stiff. And yet she says accusingly to Graham, after Frank's trickery has been revealed: 'That's another thing. I remembered with him. I don't remember with you.' The implication is that her poor memory is a defensive weapon against the disappointing past which has centred on Graham. Frank was 'pre-Dad' and puts her in touch again with the carefree Vera of her youthful days, days which she seems to have been trying to recapture. In any case, her relationship with the forceful, if insensitive and insincere Frank has caused her memory to revive with her hopes.

The vulnerable narrator, however, Graham himself, is the central focus of pity and concern. As Alan Bennett writes in his 'Introduction', he is like other narrators in *Talking Heads*, 'artless' in what he says and it is in his verbatim reports of conversation that most of the comedy of the monologue lies, although perhaps Graham is not unaware of the irony in some of the passages. He is surely aware of his mother's lack of even his own degree of sophistication when he records her saying: 'I like new experiences in eating. I had a pizza once, didn't I, Graham?' and 'Graham's quite refined. He often has a dry sherry.' But he is apparently unaware that he reveals his own limitations gradually to us. He seems to be artless, for instance, when he accepts the praise offered in a cliché by Dr Chaudhury, appreciating Graham's attempts to widen his mother's interests: 'The best way to avoid a broken hip is to have a flexible mind.' Or, for example, he thinks he is urging his mother to be more daring when he says: 'Branch out. If you can knit tea cosies you can knit skiing hats.'

Graham and his mother seem to have no friends, although the vicar calls on them, this visit resulting in one of the most amusing passages in the monologue, as Mrs Whittaker trounces the vicar's dress sense. Graham has a theological point he could make about Jesus's relationship with his Mother but, as he so often records in this tragi-comedy, he 'didn't say anything'.

One occasion when he does say something occurs at a meeting of the 'Community Caring' circle, a passage which offers an opportunity for Alan Bennett to satirise a particular kind of group therapy. 'I sometimes feel a bit out of it as I've never had any particular problems,' says Graham, with an astounding lack of self-knowledge. He takes the opportunity to discuss his anxiety about his seventy-two-year-old mother's romantic relationship, and the well-meaning social misfits in the group focus on the perception that he is, to use their jargon, 'defensive about sexual relationships'. He disagrees, but again doesn't manage to get his point across. We learn that Graham has homosexual leanings from the references to the magazines that he keeps on top of the wardrobe; he may also have had a passing interest in Joy Buckle, who taught 'Flowers in Felt and Fabric', and if so it would have been an interest probably scotched by his mother, who said Joy 'had some shocking eyebrows'. In any case, Graham seems to have constrained his sexual needs to what can be met by bedroom fantasies. He has pruned his emotional needs, too, to a minimum, but those needs are completely dependent on his relationship with his mother, as we realise when he goes so far as to plead with her, almost like a child: 'Don't go. Don't leave me, Mam.'

SUSAN in *Bed Among the Lentils*

From her narrative we discover that Susan, the disastrous wife of a trendy, ambitious vicar, is at a loss to find her role in life. 'Once upon a time,' she says, 'I had my life planned out . . . or half of it at any rate. I wasn't clear about the first part, but at the stroke of fifty I was all set to turn into a wonderful woman . . . the wife to a doctor, or a vicar's wife, Chairman of the Parish Council, a pillar of the WI.' It's the first part of her life that is causing her problems. She finds herself married to a man whose pretensions she sees through and with whom she shares neither love nor sympathy: their sexual relations are described as 'rare and desiccated conjunctions'. She doubts the religious beliefs she is assumed to have in common with her clergyman husband and resents the demands made upon her by parish duties – duties which she fulfils with a striking lack of commitment or skill.

It gradually becomes clear that her unwillingness to play a part in the life of the parish is compounded by her increasing recourse to alcohol. The first hint comes when Susan mentions that the woman at the off-licence 'didn't smile,' although, as she says, 'I spend enough'. This explains perhaps why Susan had spent the Sunday afternoon avoiding Geoffrey's company and dozing and reflecting on her wasted life, 'parked in a lay-by on the Ring Road,' when she had said she was going to deliver the parish magazine. Her accounts of embarrassing incidents when she is drunk are painfully amusing. The bishop comes to lunch (an unappetising meal of 'flabby lasagna' and tinned fruit, followed by instant coffee) in order to vet her husband for promotion, but it is clear that he is also interested in the likely contribution of Susan, to whom he refers patronisingly as 'Mrs Vicar'. Mrs Vicar fails to respond to leading questions about the ordination of women, for example, and there is a certain irony in a situation where she is being questioned about a career for women whilst in the traditional role of vicar's unpaid domestic worker. Somewhat the worse for the bottle of wine which the men did not share, she awkwardly knocks over the jug of decanted tinned milk which splashes over the bishop's gaiters. The men try to cover up her clumsiness but the bishop gives her 'a funny look' and, over instant coffee, suddenly 'remembers' that he must hurry away.

In another incident, Susan is on the rota for arranging flowers in the church. Depressed by the patronising parish workers, she fortifies herself, as is revealed later, with communion wine from the vestry. She does not appreciate the pretentious flower arrangement for the altar devised by one of the parishioners – 'a brown job, beech leaves, teazles, grass, that school of thought' – which Mrs Shrubsole calls 'Forest Murmurs'. Whilst Susan is attempting to demonstrate that the prickly bits could get in Geoffrey's eyes when he kneels at the altar, she topples over and hits her head.

The flower arrangers accompany Susan home and take the opportunity to 'conduct a fact-finding survey of all the housekeeping arrangements or absence of same', revealing that Susan's domestic accomplishments are as inadequate as her flower displays, Having sent for the vicar, the 'fan club' proceed to make a great fuss of him and, under the guise of helpfulness, undermine further Susan's shaky position.

Having slept off the effects of the communion wine, Susan goes to Leeds, to the newsagents and general shop kept by the Hindu Mr Ramesh Ramesh, where she has previously bought alcohol on various occasions and where they have struck up a friendship, sometimes talking about themselves in the back of the shop. This relationship soon has a sexual dimension and throws Susan's dissatisfaction with her husband and the Anglican Church into sharp focus. The plain vicar's wife and the attractive Asian shopkeeper talk about the Hindu religion: Ramesh has a 'Little statuette of a god on the wall. A god. Not The God. Not the definite article. One of several thousand, apparently . . . Looks a bit more fun than Jesus anyway. Shows me pictures of other gods, getting up to all sorts.' Apart from the bizarre interest of making love on a bed prepared on sacks of lentils, their sexual relationship is a revelation to Susan: obviously Ramesh has human understanding and sexual expertise undreamt of by Geoffrey. The opening words of Susan's narrative are 'Geoffrey's bad enough but I'm glad I wasn't married to Jesus.' And it is the white-clad Christ-like Ramesh – 'Like Jesus. Only not' – who is the key to her rejection of alcoholism. The Hindu Ramesh of course has all the sympathetic qualities that Susan has been unable to find in Geoffrey and Jesus, as well as a healthy enthusiasm for sex which is enhanced rather than inhibited by his religion.

Although it is Ramesh who persuades Susan to give up alcohol, her drink problem and her apparent redemption through Alcoholics Anonymous ironically provides just the career boost that Geoffrey needs: he claims the credit for supporting her through her difficulties and in the bishop's deluded view he is 'someone with a seasoned compassion, someone who's looked life in the face . . .' and the narrative ends with the prospect of certain promotion for him.

For Susan, even though she is 'much smarter . . . and seems a different woman' there is no happy ending, Unlike Alan Bennett's other 'talking heads', she has a good degree of self-knowledge, as well as a withering understanding of what she sees as the insincerity or even hypocrisy of her husband and his Church. She sees herself as unfulfilled and a failure, although she gets some bitter consolation, it seems, from her wilfully negative reactions to her situation.

The opening section sets the tone. There is an implication that Susan's mother was disappointed in her. Susan disrespectfully draws a parallel between her mother's self-martyring disposition and Jesus's agony in the

Garden of Gethsemane. Like Jesus's disciples, who slept in his hour of need, she failed to support her mother, just as she fails to support Geoffrey or the Church. Her attitude to Church traditions is clear when she says that 'if they were really sincere about religion they'd forget flower arrangement altogether, invest in some permanent plastic jobs and put the money towards the current most popular famine'. Equally, she does not see the communion wine as sacrosanct, but is pleased with herself when she suggests that cough mixture – 'it's red and sweet and nobody is going to notice' – should replace the missing wine, drunk of course by herself. Her narrative is interlaced with references to the New Testament and the Book of Common Prayer, and the last lines suggest that she is unable completely to rid herself of her belief in the Anglican God she seems to have resented all her life.

The wit and perception which she demonstrates make the tragi-comedy all the sadder, since it is clear that the personality which she reveals to those in the world of her parish has none of this vivacity and humour. She has encountered an approach to life which she admires in Ramesh Ramesh (finally living with his young wife in Preston): he has a religious ethos which can encompass uninhibited sexual enjoyment, and the ability to 'take the profit and move on'. This is something that she knows she cannot do herself. Still tied to the Anglican Church and her husband's uncongenial parishioners, she feels that her attendance at the Alcoholics Anonymous self-help meetings is just another parallel burden for her – apparently necessary but failing to meet her real needs.

MISS IRENE RUDDOCK in *A Lady of Letters*

The 'ordinary, middle-aged' Miss Irene Ruddock is a woman with a good deal of energy and we soon learn that, lacking other means of fulfilment, she takes it upon herself to report minor incidents involving people of whom she feels suspicious to their 'superiors' or the 'authorities'. Miss Ruddock, according to Alan Bennett, 'would not accept . . . that she is not a public-spirited guardian of morals' although to others she is a dangerous busybody. Letters are her means of contact with the outside world. She is lonely. Her much loved mother is dead and, after she died, Miss Ruddock received fifty-three letters. This comforting correspondence seems to have been the initial prompting for her endless interfering letters, using the pen her mother bought for her 'the last time she was able to go over to Harrogate'. 'It's been a real friend,' says Miss Ruddock: her only one, it appears. The play opens with an account of a funeral she has attended – not of a friend but of an acquaintance with whom she has spoken sometimes at the bus stop, trying to make links through the tenuous parallels in their lives. She writes to the 'director of operations' to complain of what she sees as unsatisfactory aspects of the funeral procedure and tries to extend the correspondence when he replies politely.

We learn from Miss Ruddock about various other letters she has written: to the council about a broken step; to the Queen about 'dog dirt' outside Buckingham Palace; to the press about the length of the Archbishop of Canterbury's hair; to her MP about policemen's eyesight; to sausage makers about a hair in their product. Some of her letters, for instance the one about the broken step, could be described as public-spirited, but it is clear that, at the other extreme, her correspondence verges on the unbalanced.

As in the other plays, clues about the narrator are allowed to appear gradually. Miss Ruddock gets 'a bit upset' and has to take 'tablets'. Not all her letters have been so innocent, we learn. An account of a visit from two police officers reveals that she has previously written malicious letters about local people which have caused great distress: she has, for instance, given 'the lollipop man a nervous breakdown' through her over-imaginative analysis of his character. Miss Ruddock has been before the magistrates and has been bound over to keep the peace, but subsequently she has reported the young couple living opposite her to her doctor and apparently others for neglecting their child. During the play she has been closely monitoring the activities of these neighbours but of course without ever making direct contact with them. Her reading of the situation is quite wrong and based on her suburban prejudices: the couple do not use a table-cloth; they need new curtains; the young man spends too long under his car; he wears a vest in the street and has a tattoo. When Miss Ruddock tells us that the child died not of neglect but of leukaemia, she seems strangely impassive.

After this second brush with the law, Miss Ruddock is given a suspended sentence and two social workers to counsel her. She is contemptuous of their attempts to help and dislikes their well-meaning familiarity. One of the social workers who tries to empathise with her experiences she dismisses as 'just chiming in'. The other offers suggestions for broadening her outlook and we learn a little of Miss Ruddock's philosophy of literature and life. Novels she despises for their frequently formulaic approach: when a character claims that something has never happened before (a fire, a crash, a happy ending), Miss Ruddock knows that the next thing to happen will be a fire, a crash, a happy ending. Sometimes, she tells us, she thinks that her life may be better 'next time round' but then she has to admit that she does not expect another life.

Miss Ruddock has learned nothing from her mistake over the sick child opposite. We fear the worst when she confides that the new community policeman needs reporting for keeping too good an eye on the housewife at number 56.

This final episode of busybodying, however, brings about an unexpectedly happy ending. In her final scene, in prison, Miss Ruddock, now 'Irene' to all, 'speaks very quickly and is radiant'. At last she has the opportunity to explore her potential and use up some of her drive. She rapidly masters all the courses on offer and a prospect even of a job in the real world beckons. Irene asks her tutor if when she applies for a job it will matter that she has been in prison. 'Irene', is the reply, 'with your qualifications it wouldn't matter if you'd been in the SS.'

She is friendly and supportive to a range of women, about whose crimes and life-styles she would have been very censorious in the past. Now she is understanding and sympathetic, particularly to Bridget, a prostitute who has accidentally killed her child when she was drunk.

It takes prison to break the narrow constraints of Miss Ruddock's detached existence. 'I'm that busy,' she says, in contrast to her previous life of insignificant outings and interfering letter writing. 'Prison!' she says. 'This is the first taste of freedom I've had in years'.

The balance in this short play is tilted towards comedy rather than tragedy. Miss Ruddock's blinkered view of life and her persistent state of disapproval are often humorous, as are her mistakes in etiquette and her inaccurate bad language in prison. But, like other 'talking heads', she is lonely. In her case she is isolated by the death of her mother on whom she had been dependent for a lifeline to a world beyond her bay window. A bay window, of course, offers a good view in all directions; in Miss Ruddock's case it seems also to be a barrier to other than superficial understanding of what she sees. In any case, the world beyond the window has lost the comforting qualities it used to have in earlier days, when her mother knew every family in the street. She has no friend and her only relative is 'the one cousin in Canada'. At the opening of the play she seems never to have considered a job, so she has no work-place colleagues to relate to either. The people that she meets from day to day have no real interest in her and know little about her. To the doctor she is an unfamiliar patient whose notes suggest that she can be difficult; to the vicar she is seen as a challenge to his skill in religious conversion; to the social workers she is one of many cases, perhaps hard to distinguish from each other, and dealt with in a practised, all-purpose manner which has no time to pay regard to the individual.

Given Miss Ruddock's propensity to fill her otherwise pointless life with sometimes malicious correspondence with strangers, there seems to be a tragedy in the making, and the fortunate resolution by means of a prison sentence is a dramatic twist. The narrative has led us to anticipate that Miss Ruddock will be in serious trouble with the law, but her reaction to her imprisonment is unexpected.

It is the intimacy of prison life and the women's natural supportive interest in each other that brings Irene – no longer Miss Ruddock – into a situation where she has something to offer. Instead of her usual deeply critical view of other people, she rapidly acquires tolerance, understanding and even tact. She finds a better use for her letter writing when she helps the unattractive Shirley to formulate a letter to her imaginary boyfriend, and defends Shirley against the unkind probing of Geraldine. Her cellmate is Bridget whose child has died, reminding us of the death of the child of the couple whom Irene had persecuted, although in this case the prostitute Bridget had killed her child in a drunken temper. Irene is able to accept this grim deed in a matter-of-fact way and perhaps there is a measure of atonement for her distressing lack of judgment in the case of her neighbours' sick child in that she is able to help Bridget through her nightmares about her child's death.

Her success in the courses run in prison and the possibility her qualifications offer of a life in the world outside give Irene, alone among the *Talking Heads*, the prospect of a future to look forward to.

LESLEY **in *Her Big Chance***

Alan Bennett says that Lesley, the narrator, 'thinks she has a great deal to offer as an actress and a person', implying that we should understand that she hasn't. The comedy resides in the gap between Lesley's perception of herself and her talents and our perception of her. This is the funniest of the six plays, but also perhaps the most cruel.

Lesley is a bit-part actress whose major success so far has been as an extra in Polanski's film, *Tess*, '. . . the one in the back of the farm cart wearing a shawl. The shawl was original nineteenth-century embroidery,' she adds, in an attempt to attach significance to her very minor role. For she imagines herself to be a 'serious' actress and likes to make considerable play with the need to investigate the motives of the character she is playing. She elaborates the possibilities of the one-dimensional role she is to play in the film which offers 'her big chance' and tries to discuss it with those involved as she believes it is necessary to help with the presentation of her character. 'What would help your character is if you took your bikini off,' bluntly says an assistant on the degrading film she is making for 'export video'.

The incongruous nature of her pretensions in relation to the actual demands of her role illustrates the nature of the humour throughout the piece.

Lesley also prides herself on her social skills. When she meets Spud, who is 'in films' although not at the level he suggests, at a party, 'You look an interesting person. I'm interested in interesting people. Hello,' she says, demonstrating her banal party style. She is the most transparent of all the artless narrators in this collection of short plays, and her verbatim reports of conversations make it possible for us to understand what is really going on. On this basis we can re-interpret much of what she says: what the other characters say constantly corrects Lesley's own unperceptive version. For instance, after the audition with Simon, whom Lesley at first believes to be the director of the film, she gives herself a high score of seventy-five on the basis of a chart in a book she has been reading which gives tips on interview technique. But we know that her conversation and suggestions were so inept that Simon was expressing his astonishment about her ridiculous behaviour on the telephone to someone when she made an unannounced return visit with yet more ill-judged suggestions. First she shows that she doesn't know that the film *Tess* was based on Hardy's novel. Then she drops Polanski's name and says that they had a very open relationship (she was an extra). This gives Simon a chance to turn to the subject of the role of Travis in the film. Travis, too, he says is very open. His sarcasm is plain when he adds that she is an 'interesting' character who 'spends most of the film on the deck of a yacht'. Lesley foolishly suggests that there is a link here with the small power boat her brother-in-law keeps at Ipswich. 'Well! Snap!' says Simon, with a heavy irony which we know is completely missed by the unaware Lesley. This pattern is repeated throughout the narrative.

Her pretensions and her pert, silly style mean that she is left well alone socially by most of the film crew. Even those who have been to bed with her do not reappear in her narrative. When the rest of those involved in the film are out together in the evenings, they go to the restaurant run by Lesley's stand-in for the water skiing, whom Lesley took at first to be a part-time waitress. This 'ginger' girl is the only other female mentioned and it is easy to see that her company, like that of almost anyone, would be preferable to that of foolish and boring Lesley.

Lesley's vanity does not extend to what is obviously her very real physical attraction: once Gunther, the director, has seen her naked he seems to mark her out as his prey, a situation perhaps reflected by the cat watching the trout in the animal handler's bedroom. It is, though, only on the last night that he goes to bed with her, no doubt in order to make sure that he will not have to see her again.

As well as being constantly out of her depth in understanding what is going on around her, Lesley suffers the lack of self-knowledge that afflicts most of the narrators of these plays and doesn't accept that all she has to offer as an 'actress' is an attractive and photogenic body. Just as sadly, her misjudged social skills send the film team scuttling away from her as they, too, have no use for her company and 'serious' conversation, although individually they are only too willing to take advantage of her physical charms.

The play ends at a point before the first scene (see section on time and place in *Talking Heads*). Lesley reveals that she is planning to enrich her life still further so that she will have even more to give as an actress.

Nevertheless, one of her possible additional skills might be 'selling valuable oil paintings', something we know is beyond her but which reflects her acceptance that she might need to earn a living by other means than acting.

But the first scene, which was set a week or so after the end of the play, shows Lesley in brashly bright mood again, having worked out what she would consider a challenging remark to engage interest: 'I shot a man last week . . .'

MURIEL in *Soldiering On*

Even though Muriel Carpenter says that she is not 'a tragic woman', her life has a considerable tragic dimension. The decline in her fortunes from the comfort of her position at the beginning of the play to her friendless, pauper state at the end has the hallmarks of a small-scale tragedy.

In the first scene she is meeting the loss of her obviously energetic and well-known husband bravely. 'Ralph touched life at many points,' said the vicar at his funeral, and Muriel has had to entertain the many mourners who have come to pay their last respects. She describes her well-practised preparations for the late lunch with touches of humour, but with pride, too, in her capacity to 'manage' in difficult circumstances. She is confident of her organising ability.

Her shock and grief are very real and she tries to do all the 'right things', following practices that Ralph would have recommended. Advice on bereavement seems to be in short supply – the receptionist at the health centre, for instance, said that they had had some pamphlets but offered the feeble excuse that they had not bothered to re-order because children scribbled on them. However, she has no difficulty in disposing of Ralph's things: charity organisers descend on her rapaciously with requests for his clothes, shoes, books – even his spectacles.

Of their two children, Giles and Margaret, Giles is obviously his mother's favourite. Margaret, we learn, is another of the characters in *Talking Heads* who have to take 'tablets' because they have mental health problems. Always her father's favourite and 'little girl', why does she believe, we wonder, that her father has been killed and a little later waits in the hall in her outdoor clothes with her bag packed, claiming to be waiting for the police.

Giles seems at first to be helping his mother over her finances. Ralph, who never discussed money matters, has left her 'very nicely off' and has 'tied up a bit for Margaret'. Muriel deceives herself over Giles's character, but we soon become aware that he is helping himself to her money and that his investments on her behalf are not only unwise but disastrous. As scene follows scene, poor Muriel is reduced to cutting down on expenses, putting Margaret into an institution, then finally selling up in order to live in a boarding-house 'flatlet' at Hunstanton. She suffers severe loneliness and poverty, which she meets with her all-purpose fortitude.

She is pleased, however, that Margaret is now so much better that she is like 'a normal daughter' and comes to take her mother out to lunch – with no ulterior motive, unlike that of Giles, whose purpose in taking his mother out to lunch earlier in the play was to make her slightly confused so that he could persuade her to let him take control of her funds. Nevertheless, Muriel has had to digest the knowledge that her daughter's illness was caused by her father's abuse of his 'little girl' – knowledge which she seems able to accept with her usual stoicism. Margaret, she says, 'Doesn't blame him. Wishes he were alive. Don't know what I think. Sorry for him, I suppose.' Alan Bennett writes, 'Muriel ends up knowing her husband ruined her daughter but is no closer to realising that she had a hand in it too.' We become aware that her pride in her military-style organisation of family life and her 'soldiering on' attitude to problems disguises her lack of perception in relationships and her failure to distinguish major from minor problems in life. It is Ralph, of course, who has been her mentor: 'It doesn't matter if you're going to get married, commit a burglary or keep a guinea pig; efficiency is the proper collation of information.'

It seems that, although she has been a capable housewife and the competent partner of an army officer and business executive, she has not really known the members of her family. She has been unaware of Ralph's preying upon his child, or of Giles's duplicitous nature. Her interest in Margaret seems to have been just about below the level of her interest in the dogs: after the funeral she does not get up at night to see to Margaret, who is disturbed, until she remembers that she has not fed the dogs. After the financial disaster, Margaret is sent to an institution and the dogs soon have to go too.

Unlike the rest of the narrators in *Talking Heads*, Muriel, at the opening of the play, is used to a comfortable middle-class life with her days passed in enjoyable activity. She has educated tastes, we guess from her interest in architecture and her hope that she might be able to go to Siena. She is used to having plenty to offer and is an experienced organiser of voluntary work and charity money-raiser. There are many ironies in the development of the play: she does maintain her ability to 'soldier on', but no other aspect of her former life seems to be useful to her in her new, difficult circumstances.

Previously Muriel has found a sense of community and companionship through the charities network; in the final scene we learn that she is considered only as a possible recipient of help. The fact that she strenuously declines – 'Not on your life' – shows not only her dismay at the clerk's mistake but also reveals that she must view those who receive benefits or charitable help as unacceptable socially. We know that she will continue somehow on a starvation diet rather than join those who have to depend on society's support.

There is irony, too, in the fact that Margaret is actually successfully treated in the overcrowded and inconvenient National Health psychiatric hospital. The well-kept lawns and good quality cup of tea in matron's room at the private nursing home regretted by Muriel may well have been the pleasant façade of a régime that knew it would have been inadvisable to discover the cause of Margaret's illness – a discreet approach that would have protected Ralph but was of no use to his daughter.

And in the end the journey Muriel makes is to Hunstanton, which is a far cry from the journey she had thought of making to the historic and architecturally beautiful Siena.

Muriel's world has let her down: the financial disaster caused by Giles has revealed how little she had of lasting value in her life. Only her betrayed daughter seems to have time for her and it is no wonder that she escapes from the unrewarding present by watching television or putting on her earphones.

DORIS in *A Cream Cracker Under the Settee*

Frail elderly Doris has had a fall whilst wilfully dusting out of reach, strictly against the orders of her home-help, Zulema. We are in effect sharing her last hours. Doris is too houseproud and obsessed with cleanliness. Alan Bennett writes that 'though she knows it's her determination to dust that's brought about her downfall, what she doesn't see is that it's the same obsession that tidied her husband into the grave.'

Her fall has left her in a serious condition – her leg or hip is badly injured – yet she is still fussing about the gate being left open, letting in dogs and 'all sorts', and the neighbours' leaves in her front garden. Wilfred, her husband, was allowed a small non-deciduous bush in the garden, although Doris would have preferred concrete, in spite of Wilfred's suggestion that concrete has no character, She recalls that she said, 'Never mind character, Wilfred, where does hygiene come on the agenda? With concrete you can feel easy in your mind.' However, all Wilfred's other plans fail to come to fruition: Doris seems to have dampened his enthusiasm for growing mushrooms in the cellar, making fretwork toys, and having an allotment.

Doris's view of cleanliness and hygiene restricts her whole outlook on life. She knows that beyond her doorstep her own spotless regime does not operate – even the front garden is subject to urinators and neighbours' leaves. In Stafford House, the old people's home that beckons, she fears that not only would she be forced to socialise, but she imagines the inmates 'smelling of pee'. There is a time dimension to her obsession, too – the past was different: '. . .people were clean and the streets were clean

and it was all clean . . .' Like many old people, she looks back regretfully
to what she sees as a golden age; the present for her lacks what she values
and she does not at all appreciate what the present does offer, that is, a
home help and the prospect of care in an old people's home. Zulema, the
cheery sounding home-help, she sees as an adversary to be challenged and,
if possible, defeated: 'She wants reporting,' Doris says after her trium-
phant discovery of the half-hidden cream cracker Zulema has missed. And
of course Stafford House, which Zulema describes in optimistic terms, is
not to be countenanced at any cost. Doris gives a hilarious account of
her idea of the horrors of having to mix – when it is not only the 'old
lasses' but the clothes and even the teeth that are mixed up. She says,
'You go daft there, there's nowhere else for you to go but daft,' as she
imagines a scene of tambourine-banging and organised chants of 'I am
H.A.P.P.Y.'

'A kiddy'd've solved all that,' Doris says of Wilfred's half-hearted
intentions to take up hobbies. It would have solved her immediate
problems too, she thinks, as she imagines her baby having lived and
produced grandchildren for her: 'Wouldn't have been in this fix'.

Doris's brief account of the birth of her apparently stillborn baby is
central to the play. The midwife took the baby away without letting Doris
see him and wrapped him in paper, 'As if he was dirty'. Doris's instincts
were that 'He wasn't dirty, little thing,' showing that at that time she was
able to respond to birth, one of the very messiest of events, with a normal
human acceptance. The grief and disappointment seem to have marked a
'before and after' division in Doris's life. The sadness of the loss of the
baby is brought back to Doris as she remembers the never used pram,
bought over-confidently in advance by Wilfred, and foreshadowing his
subsequent failure to follow through any of his plans. Doris's crusade
against dirt must have developed obsessively after the failure of their
hopes of family life with its demands on the acceptance of a measure of
mess and disorder. Now, at the end of her life, she looks back to a
time when cleanliness was associated with happiness – the time before the
baby's death. Not only were the streets and the people in them clean, there
was a friendliness she remembers and now misses, and married life meant
contentment: 'I'd wash up while he read the paper and we'd eat the toffees
and listen to the wireless . . .'

Perhaps at the end of the play Doris does accept that, in the absence of
any relatives, society in general has been trying to look after her. She
thanks the concerned policeman who has been checking up on her one
more time than is necessary. But, of course, it is a crucial 'No! Thank you'
for Doris, as we understand that she is stating her intention to die alone
rather than end her days in the dreaded Stafford House.

As she begins to drift in and out of consciousness, she goes back to her
childhood and her earliest recollections of the association of happiness

with cleanliness: 'I wish I was ready for bed. All washed and in a clean nightie and the bottle in, all sweet and crisp and clean . . .'

The unseen characters

The characters and motives of the central narrators have already been discussed. But beyond the central narrators of each of the plays, many other characters spring to life in *Talking Heads*. The detailed accounts of events given by each narrator include, in particular, a representation of conversations that is intended to sound like verbatim reporting of what was said. This feature of Alan Bennett's story-telling is most effective in peopling his plays. There is also some straightforward description and comment on the narrators' attitudes to the unseen characters.

We must be aware, of course, of prejudice on the part of the narrators in what we are being told. As Alan Bennett says in his 'Introduction', we do not have an objective view of what is going on and some of the unseen characters, as well as being misunderstood, as in the case of Lesley's assessments, may also be maligned. This is an obvious implication of the single viewpoint in each monologue.

In *A Chip in the Sugar*, for instance, Graham in his account would like to think of his mother as a frail and forgetful old lady, very dependent upon her son for practicalities, as well as deferring to him in the formation of her tastes and attitudes to society. We can easily see, however, that even if physically a bit feeble – although rather livelier than Graham suggests – she is spirited and adaptable and still looking for adventure at seventy-two. In the interests of her own desire for what would be perhaps a last fling, it is clear that she is prepared to sacrifice Graham's need for stability.

Vicars do not come off well in these stories, as the dramatist acknowledges in the 'Introduction', and Mrs Whittaker trounces the clergyman who steps into her sitting room, collecting money for famine relief. The conversation, re-enacted by Graham, is really between the vicar and Mrs Whittaker, with Graham very much sidelined: she has a ready line in repartee while Graham of course tells us that, frequently, he 'didn't say anything'. The vicar serves the purpose of demonstrating Mrs Whittaker's inclination to dominate, and also that the household's callers are formal representatives of society, rather than friends or relatives. He is deftly sketched in, though, in the account Graham gives, as trendy, earnest and superficially interested in his parishioners.

Frank Turnbull, it is easy to suspect, must have a great deal more about him than Graham allows. Their dislike of each other is partly fought out on sartorial grounds – each despising the other's style of dress. Turnbull finds Graham's socks, sandals and plastic mac unacceptable and Graham thinks Turnbull looks like a bookmaker in his flashy, over-colourful outfits. Turnbull is brash and reactionary but he has a zest for life that Graham certainly lacks. Until his daughter reveals his deception it is clear that he has easily won the battle for the allegiance of Mrs Whittaker. As Alan Bennett says, Graham does not realise that he is as good as married to his mother, but the story he tells is a rather grotesque version of a familiar type of domestic drama, with Mrs Whittaker the erring wife, Graham the dull husband and Frank Turnbull the dashing seducer. That the players in this eternal triangle are rather different from what might be expected adds to the comedy, of course, and disguises the pathos of the situation.

Another dimension is added to our understanding of Graham by his account of a session of 'Community Caring', involving informal group therapy. The characters of Steve, who runs the group, and Leonard, Janice and Jackie, his 'clients', are barely differentiated: they serve the purpose of reminding us of Graham's mental illness and the support that society tries to offer – a support which is not valued by Graham. He is unable to face a discussion about his mother's intended marriage in what seems to him the distasteful terminology of the group. The parody of social work is one of the funniest episodes in this monologue.

Susan, in *Bed Among the Lentils*, is such an engaging character that it is difficult not to take her assessment of Geoffrey at face value. But it does occur to us that Geoffrey, too, is having a difficult time, with a wife who questions the sincerity of the Church and her role as vicar's helpmeet. We accept that Geoffrey is ambitious, but perhaps do not see his desire for a career as wrong in itself; it is hard not to see the dreadful lunch with the bishop from his point of view, too – awful food and an uncommitted wife who is drunk as well.

The characters introduced to us through Susan's narration are mostly those whom she sees as part of the burden she has to bear as Geoffrey's wife. If she makes no effort for the bishop – sketched in as a hearty, forthright man who, she knows, holds considerable power – she has still less to offer to parishioners. We are given glimpses of Mr and Mrs Belcher, who Susan suggests are puffed up with pride because both are involved in a Sunday service; Miss Budd and Miss Bantock, imagined in a fumbling lesbian encounter, as unsatisfactory as marital relations at the vicarage; and of course the flower-arranging ladies, Mrs Belcher again, Miss Frobisher and the formidable Mrs Shrubsole. The incident involving 'Forest Murmurs', Susan's drunken fall, and the subsequent opportunities for interference by the ladies of the parish, is very entertaining and also encapsulates all that Susan finds pointless and petty about her life in the parish, and the alliance of her husband with what she calls his 'fans' emphasises her isolation. What seems like something of a conspiracy between Geoffrey and his sycophantic flock could just reflect their difficulties in knowing what to do about Susan's alcoholism, although the malicious interpretation that Susan puts on it is much more amusing.

Few characters as seen through the eyes of the narrators come over as admirable except for Ramesh Ramesh. He, of course, is an exotic creation, not only for his oriental religious philosophy and lack of sexual inhibitions, but also for his suggestion of an alternative way of life from that in which Susan feels herself imprisoned – he is able to 'take the profit and move on', something which Susan feels she should be able to do but knows she will not.

Until Irene Ruddock finds herself in enforced contact with other women when she is sent to prison, she has no friends. She is a great letter writer and watcher of other people. Her prejudices against the young couple opposite are based only on visual impressions; her judgment seems all the more unkind when we learn of their child's fatal illness. The police who call about her interfering she tries to keep at arm's length, although she avoids direct condemnation of them. Her two social workers' attempts to help are, however, mercilessly criticised. She despises what she sees as their clumsy efforts to understand her situation and to alleviate her isolation; the appearance of one of them, too – 'looks more in need of social work than I do' – attracts her contempt.

When the self-imposed constraint of her everyday life is changed for the real physical confinement of prison, Miss Ruddock enjoys a dramatic change in her view of her fellow-humans. The disparagingly described vicar, magistrate and social workers give way to sympathetically observed criminals. While she approves of her prison education tutors, Mrs Proctor, Miss Macaulay and Mrs Dunlop, she can also describe some of her fellow inmates with warmth and understanding. Amazingly, she is 'friends with practically everyone' – Lucille; obese, confused Shirley; and pretty Bridget, her cellmate, who has murdered her child. These characters spring to sympathetic life in Irene's narration as what seemed likely to be a dire future for her turns into an unexpected happy ending.

In *Her Big Chance* we are in the seedy world of third-rate film-making. 'Actress' could be only a courtesy title for Lesley, whose experience has previously been limited to playing film extras or walk-on television parts. Her function as 'Travis' in a cheap sex and violence film we soon see is to provide nude scenes. She is unable to cope with the few lines written in the script for her, although she does not realise this. We feel almost sorry for the harassed film crew who have to deal with her pretensions and lack of acting ability. Lesley 'collects' people, we learn at the beginning of the monologue, and she presents her collection – the film crew – to us one by one: Spud, the electrician; Simon, the general assistant; Scott, in charge of wardrobe and make-up; Nigel, the director's assistant; Terry, a cameraman; Kenny, the animal handler; and Gunther, the director. Those who want to are able to get into bed with her: the cynical preliminaries are naïvely related to us by Lesley, who obviously thinks that she is recording vivacious, interesting conversations that she has with the predatory Spud, Terry, Kenny and Gunther. Predictably, none of them pursues her acquaintance.

The characters who are not interested in her physical charms are sometimes verbally quite scathing, although Lesley is not perceptive enough to spot this. Simon is sarcastic, although she does not see it, but he lets her down lightly when he gets rid of her at the end of the audition, saying of her extravagant suggestions about Travis, 'I'm most grateful. You've given me a lot of ideas,' but we understand only too well that his politeness covers a relief that she is going. Scott, the embittered wardrobe man, is very cutting – even Lesley realises this – but she puts this down to his personal problems and is thus able to ignore what he says. Nigel, the director's assistant, is apparently used to handling actresses' inflated ideas of their talents; we can see from Lesley's reported conversations during filming that she is driving him to breaking point when she thinks she is being constructive. Eventually, he is unable to maintain a reasonable civility and says coarsely, 'Who do you think you're playing, Emily Brontë? Gunther wants to see your knockers.'

Lesley tells us at the beginning of *Her Big Chance* that her professionalism requires her to be involved in her work; she seems to think that she is giving an intelligent account of the way in which she has forged relationships with the members of the team, and has contributed to the development of the director's vision. Since her account is perceived to be entirely illusionary, the secondary characters in this play greatly influence our coming to a more realistic understanding of the story.

At the opening of *Soldiering On* Muriel Carpenter, surrounded by friends and acquaintances, seems to view them mainly in terms of management or organisation. The mourners at Ralph's funeral have to be fed afterwards. Muriel is in charge, but she is appreciative of the efforts of those she sees as assistant organisers – Mabel, her housekeeper or home help, who has produced a soup that sounds rather dull, and family who help out with guided tours and polite conversations. Muriel, in spite of her grief, introduces people to each other without necessarily knowing them herself. She and Mabel in a brief interlude have 'a good laugh and a good cry' before 'hurling themselves back into the fray'. It is all rather like an army exercise. And so is the way in which Muriel is always prepared to move on in response to circumstances. It is clear that Mabel has been with her for a long time – she has had to polish the furniture 'all these years' and is aware of Margaret's precarious state of health. But Muriel, although perhaps suggesting that Mabel may now be looking for a husband, moves on, as though to another 'posting', with no further comment.

Of Muriel's fellow workers for charity who descend on the house like locusts in the battle for charity shop items from amongst Ralph's belongings, only Angela stands out. The first reference to her is of 'awful Angela

Gillespie'; she advises Muriel about the disposal of the 'jumble', buys a long fancied corner cupboard at the auction, says what everyone but Muriel has known about crooked Giles, but 'awful Angela' remains the only person from the 'old days' still in touch with Muriel at the end of the story. We cannot tell whether this is a further trial for Muriel or whether she now sees Angela in a different light. In rather the same way, the young psychiatrist of whom Muriel disapproves is able to help Margaret towards a cure. Also, it is her undervalued daughter who is in touch with her mother by the end of the narrative, and not her dreadful favourite, Giles.

Giles is one of the few real villains to appear in *Talking Heads* and the tension is heightened by his mother's falure to realise how little he cares for her and how cellously she is being exploited. The smug safety of his own life contrasts painfully at the end with Muriel's impoverishment, and his pretended distress at her position results in what must be the final blow – the loss of contact with her grandchildren. Margaret, on the contrary, moves from the kind of sub-human status Muriel affords her at the beginning of her narrative into a warm, human dimension. Ralph remains something of a mystery: much loved and yet little known by his wife; a figure widely respected in the world and a betrayer of his family at home – perhaps we recognise him as one of those bafflingly kindly wrongdoers who figure in the crime pages of the press.

Muriel has been a successful hostess and partner to an ex-officer and senior business executive; when she can deal with people in familiar, conventional social situations she is in her element. When these patterns cease to exist – family life with Ralph at its head, the mistress–servant relationship, the voluntary work hierarchy – she is in a world for which she is unprepared and in which her lack of real judgment and understanding of people becomes apparent. The unseen characters in this monologue spring to life as they do in the other plays, although there is less verbatim re-enacting of conversation – it would not be Muriel's style. We get more reported conversation and straightforward narrative. Alan Bennett shows the same skill, however, in using these characters to reveal much of what we know about the central narrator.

Wilfred and Zulema, even though invisible, play the supporting roles in *A Cream Cracker Under the Settee*. Another of Alan Bennett's lonely characters, without friends or relatives, Doris spends much of her time in the play in remembering her husband, Wilfred, and their earlier married days. Wilfred comes over as good-natured and even dominant in the first stage of their marriage – he insists on buying the bargain perambulator before the baby is born. We soon realise, however, that at some point in their life after the disappointment about the baby Wilfred's spirit has been broken. He does not carry through any of his plans and Doris never imagines for a moment that her interest in hygiene and cleanliness could have been destructive for Wilfred. Even in what we know will be her final hours she shows a keen interest in Zulema's cleaning, or lack of it. If thoughts of Wilfred provide Doris's only remaining link with a world that she once found kindly, Zulema represents the world 'outside' from which Doris now shrinks.

Zulema represents the forces of society at large, which have taken on responsibility for Doris, very much against her will. 'Outside' are the neighbours, unknown and often changing; dirty little boys; tiresome religious cranks. With them she includes the dreaded Stafford House – the old people's home which inevitably lies in wait, perhaps the policeman who keeps an eye on her, and certainly Zulema, the agent of the social services in her eyes. Looking past Doris's prejudiced description of Zulema, we can see a well-intentioned home help, who offers sensible advice to Doris and probably cleans up well enough. She is friendly and cheerful and tries to make Doris see that Stafford House is not the awful place she believes it to be. We can also tell, of course, that Doris is only one of many elderly or infirm people that Zulema must visit in the course of a week, and that her interest in Doris would have to be described as professional.

Unlike some of the other short plays, *A Cream Cracker Under the Settee* is thinly populated, but, as in the other monologues, the unseen characters play a crucial role in our understanding of the narrator. Here Wilfred and Zulema may seem very different figures in her household and yet each of them she sees as enemies in her endless battle over dust and dirt.

Monologue as tragi-comedy

The literary term for each of these plays is monologue or monodrama. The terms refer to a single person speaking alone. Most prayers and poetic laments are monologues, as are soliloquies – usually self-examination or self-revelation, as in, for example, *Hamlet* or *Othello*. A monodrama is a monologue in the form of a play in which there is only one character, for example, *Krapp's Last Tape*, by Samuel Beckett (1906–89). (For those who are interested in exact terminology, the plays in *Talking Heads* can well be described as monopolylogues, since, in each, one performer plays many parts in re-enacting past conversations.)

Each of the above definitions can be seen as relevant to a study of *Talking Heads*: for instance, we recognise the lament that lies beneath the narrator's story, as we recognise the self-revelation if not the self-examination of the Shakespearean soliloquy. Perhaps because in a literary sense we are trained to accept the monologue, the strangeness of our relationship to the narrator is not at first apparent. In the first place, whom is the narrator addressing? In *Soldiering On* Muriel Carpenter at the end says, 'I wouldn't want you to think this was a tragic story,' making 'you' or us identified confidantes of her story. Otherwise, a viewer/listener/reader is not identified. Indeed, the whole problem for these mostly lonely or isolated people is that they have no one in whom to confide. This puts a viewer into the position of a *voyeur*, or an eavesdropper. Although in no cases do the narrators examine their own responsibilities for their unsatisfactory position in the world, nevertheless their transparency in revealing themselves unwittingly to the viewer suggests an invasion of privacy. This leaves the viewer, who is probably helpless with laughter – for the plays are very funny – nevertheless feeling uneasy. With the exception of Susan, the very self-aware vicar's wife, the characters' intended purpose is not to provoke laughter but somehow to justify themselves, to call attention to their plight. Alan Bennett manipulates our response first by making us laugh and then by making us accept that, in the end, the lives of these characters are no laughing matter, unless we take the view that in any case life is something of a comical charade, and that we, too, inevitably show symptoms of what is after all probably only the natural human condition.

An aspect of the monologue which is well worth bearing in mind is that it has often been used to serve the purposes of comedy. Music hall turns in the first half of the twentieth century included monologues or recitations which could be seriously intended but which, much more often, were humorous: a favourite was Stanley Holloway's (1890–1982) *Albert and the Lion*. Later in the century artistes such as Mabel Constanduros (*d.* 1957 'aged 77') and Joyce Grenfell (1910–79) developed music hall and revue turns which were much more subtle. Joyce Grenfell's one woman show could be seen as anticipating a *Talking Head* in that her characters invariably had the 'artlessness' which Alan Bennett describes as being a major attribute of his narrators. This meant that her audience apparently understood more of what was happening on stage than did the person she was portraying, who might be a kindergarten teacher, for example, or a music lover. Her characters were not touched by tragedy, however, and there was a comfortable collusion between author and audience over what was going on.

Monologues such as those of Joyce Grenfell had central characters who were middle-class, often mildly pretentious, and the resulting humour was gentle. Other comedians provided more robust fare, and a performer such as Norman Evans (*d.* 1962 'aged 61') and his act *Over the Garden Wall* could also be seen as a forerunner of *Talking Heads*. His favourite character, an elderly woman with unstable teeth and bosom, who always appeared as though with her elbows resting on a back-garden wall, was very crudely sketched and much of the comedy relied on *double entendre*. However, 'her' incongruous juxtaposition of ideas and re-enacting of sharp conversations find at least an echo in the style of Alan Bennett's short plays.

In *A Chip in the Sugar*, for example, Graham's mother is the source of many a snappy conversation that would make material for a stand-up comedian (an entertainer who relies for comic effect on his particular way of delivering jokes and anecdotes). Graham reports an exchange she has had with the vicar, when she asks him where he got his shoes. He says: ' "They're training shoes." She said, "Training for what? Are you not fully qualified?" He said, "If Jesus were alive today, Mrs Whittaker, I think you'd find these were the type of shoes he would be wearing." "Not if his mother had anything to do with it," she said. "She'd have him down Stead and Simpson's and get him some good brogues." '

A vicar is at the receiving end again in *A Lady of Letters* when Miss Ruddock challenges his proffered cross as a means of identification since, as she says, even hooligans now wear them, possibly in their ears.

Doris, also, in *A Cream Cracker Under the Settee*, rehearses a pert conversation with Zulema after she finds the cracker that Zulema has failed to notice in her evidently sketchy cleaning. Wilfred, too, has been the recipient in the past of some telling remarks about the nature of concrete and hygiene.

All three of these doughty ladies have a combative style and a turn of phrase that many a music-hall entertainer would recognise as guaranteeing comic success. This knockabout stuff, however, is only one of the weapons in Alan Bennett's writer's armoury: his comedy arises from many sources. In *Bed Among the Lentils* Susan, the vicar's wife, is a witty woman and unlike the other narrators in that she is very self-aware, even though this does not prevent her from being trapped in an unhappy situation from which she is unable to escape. The sense of unease that creeps into what can seem like an intrusion into privacy in relation to some of the characters does not operate here, and Susan's subversive questioning and cynical assessments of others' motives are purely enjoyable. We can relish the posers she presents to her self-seeking husband by suggesting that cough mixture will serve perfectly well as an emergency substitute for communion wine, for instance, or by asking him if he thinks Jesus ever 'smirked'. She tells the tale of the flower arranging with a pointed wit, as amused by her own dire role in the incident as by the account of the pretensions of Mrs Shrubsole's 'Forest Murmurs' and the sycophancy of what she calls the vicar's 'fans'. Amusing, too, is her recording of her sexual encounters with the handsome Mr Ramesh Ramesh by marking the occasions with reference to parallel events on the Church calendar; a particularly satisfactory meeting, for instance, she mentions as having taken place amongst the lentils on the second Sunday after Trinity, and yet another on the feast of St Simon and St Jude. She is, it seems, enjoying a private, idiosyncratic revenge upon Geoffrey and the Church.

The humour in the remaining two plays is more to do with the situation of the central characters. In the case of *Soldiering On*, Muriel Carpenter is aware of the ironic humour of her position, which we can share, although, as Alan Bennett says, she fails to realise in which ways she has contributed to her difficulties. She gives a wryly humorous account of the charity scavengers who descend upon her in search of loot in the form of her late husband's clothes, books, shoes and so on; later, a similar group of people arrive at the auction of her house and contents, keen once again to benefit from her misfortunes. The vicar and her friend, Angela, for instance, each has an eye on particular pieces of furniture they have long coveted, a walnut sidetable and the corner cupboard respectively. Muriel's recognition that her organising skills are no longer in demand is told, too, with a bitter humour when she offers her services to the community in the small town to which she has moved, only for it to be assumed that she is asking for assistance rather than offering it. As she says: '. . . message received and understood. The old girl's past it.'

Her Big Chance is a very funny play in which the ridiculous narrator completely fails to understand what is going on in the events which she describes. Poor Lesley thinks that she is a perceptive actress and a well-developed individual. Her naïve re-enacting of the many conversations she has during her audition and brief filming experience show that in each case she is judged and found wanting. Ignorant, pretentious, incompetent – her inadequacies are brutally revealed through her comic misjudgments of the success of her social and professional encounters. The humour in this play is destructive and withholds our sympathy from the narrator in a way that is not evident in the other *Talking Heads*.

Comedy of one sort or another is very much to the fore in these plays, but each has a tragic dimension as well. Tragedy is not perhaps a word readily associated with the situations of the narrators in *Talking Heads*. In dramatic terms it belongs traditionally to heroic plays about the downfall of the great: Oedipus or Agamemnon are classic figures of Greek tragedy, Othello and King Lear are examples of Shakespeare's great tragic figures. Graham, Susan, Irene, Lesley, Muriel, Doris . . . do they belong in that company? They are little people. Yet modern works have brought an acceptance that ordinary people can be the subjects of tragic drama, following great nineteenth-century dramatists such as Ibsen (1828–1906) or Chekhov (1860–1904), whose tragi-comedies create the same kind of emotional confusion of which Alan Bennett is a contemporary master. In this century, Tennessee Williams (1911–83), for instance, has produced searing images of tragic provincial life, and Brecht's (1898–1956) *Mother Courage* or Arthur Miller's (*b.* 1915) *Death of a Salesman* offer memorable examples of the tragedies of little people. Miller's defeated salesman, Willy Loman, in fact demands the same kind of attention from the audience as do Alan Bennett's narrators: 'Attention, attention must be finally paid to such a person,' insists his wife. The narrators of *Talking Heads* demand the same of us.

Time and place

Alan Bennett's approach to settings and chronology seems to be consistent in the monologues, and yet within the obvious constraints of the form he has rung the changes to suit each narrator's story. The time scale, for instance, varies from one short day, in *A Cream Cracker Under the Settee*, to a considerable length of time, perhaps a year, in *Bed Among the Lentils*. Equally, so far as the settings are concerned, he limits the telling of the narrative in *A Chip in the Sugar* to Graham's bedroom, whereas in *Her Big Chance* there is a widening out from the opening setting of Lesley's flat to scenes where she is between work sessions on the film.

Graham's room in *A Chip in the Sugar* is spartan, a single man's room, and this is the background to his story throughout the play. The humour, as usual, is balanced by the bleakness of the narrator's situation, and we find ourselves in a really quite painful kind of intimacy with his problems. This tension is created not least by the claustrophobic setting. His room is Graham's refuge, evidently, a place where he can be safe, but it becomes clear during the play that he feels besieged there, too. The house is being watched and he is disturbed not only by the fear of being observed but also by the fear that his oppressive illness is returning. And, of course, his mother's marriage will mean the loss of his home and his room.

The play proceeds chronologically, like an occasional diary. There are five scenes, the first a long account of Mrs Whittaker's meeting in the town in northern England where they live with Frank Turnbull, a friend from the 'old days'. The other scenes, over an unidentified time scale of probably a few weeks, reveal the development of the romance and its ending when Frank's deception is uncovered. Two of these scenes are described as being at night: the fourth scene, in which Graham is sitting in his pyjamas on his unmade bed, marks his point of deepest despair, and the night setting and his inability to sleep add to this mood. The final scene is also at night, but Graham, his confidence returned, has been reading one of his magazines and then sits comfortably in his easy chair. His life has resumed its precarious balance and, for the time being, all is well again. No imaginary person has been watching the house, but a real person has delivered him from his predicament; the symptoms of his illness have not returned; his mother is restored to him.

In *Bed Among the Lentils* Alan Bennett goes rather further afield in his settings and the time span of the narrative is considerable. There are scenes in the country church near Leeds, in the vestry and in the side chapel; in the vicarage there are two scenes in the kitchen and the final one in the drawing room. The church scenes support central incidents in the monologue: in the side chapel Susan is polishing a candlestick, a reference to her duties in the church and perhaps to the later flower arranging débâcle. The vestry, the cupboard door now locked, was one of Susan's sources of alcohol in the form of the communion wine. Alan Bennett uses the vicarage scenes to show Susan's reformation (probably temporary) as the careless drunkard of the kitchen becomes the now perfectly presentable smart woman of the drawing room.

The clues to the time span of this monologue show that the five scenes take place over quite a period of time, probably about a year. Appropriately, the dramatist charts the events by means of dates in the Church calendar. Susan's first scene describes events before Easter; the fourth scene dates a memorable visit to Ramesh Ramesh as taking place on the second Sunday after Trinity (June); and the fifth refers to another visit to Ramesh on the feast of St Simon and St Jude (28 October), although since that time Susan has undergone probably quite lengthy treatment for alcoholism and 'seems a different woman'. The use of dates from the Church calendar marks time conveniently and it also makes an ironic comment, considering the nature of Susan's activities.

There is a marked dramatic twist at the end of *A Lady of Letters* and the sets support the plot. Most of the play's seven scenes take place in Miss Ruddock's sitting room in a town in northern England, as she pursues her self-appointed duty of observing her neighbours; the room is her centre of operations and Alan Bennett creates the impression in the first four scenes that when she is not on the look-out she is busy at her letter writing. The following scene, forwarding the plot, is set at the police station, or perhaps at the social services office. Miss Ruddock is in her outdoor clothes and has had what we learn is a second brush with the law. In the sixth scene – the last but one – Miss Ruddock is back at home but we suspect that her suspended sentence will come into force when she becomes over-curious about the new policeman's pattern of calls.

Sure enough, in the last scene Miss Ruddock, now Irene, is in prison, although to our surprise she is revelling in the opportunities prison life offers her. The settings have helped to support the narrative: in particular Miss Ruddock's displacement from her own room to the police station in the third scene prepares us to some extent for her sudden imprisonment in the final one. In some scenes time of day is not mentioned, otherwise it is daytime except for the sombre fourth scene, set at dusk, which precedes her arrest and in which Miss Ruddock explains her feeling that the street nowadays is full of strangers who do not keep an eye on the neighbourhood.

The time scale seems to be linked to the unknown sick child who lives opposite Miss Ruddock. The first scene refers to the young family having just moved in; subsequent scenes show Miss Ruddock's disquiet about the family; we are told of the death of the child in the fifth scene; finally in the seventh scene references to Irene's cellmate Bridget's dead child offer an echo of the young neighbours' tragedy. The time scale linking the dead children matters: Irene is a changed character in the final scene and her understanding attitude to Bridget's guilt and horror about her dead child serves as an illustration of her redemption.

The first two and the last scenes in *Her Big Chance* are set in Lesley's flat in Bromley and serve as a frame, representing her normal everyday life. In the third and fourth scenes, the opportunity is taken to show Lesley waiting to work on the film she sees as an opportunity to impress with her imaginary acting skills. The small, bleak dressing-room and the anonymous hotel room specified serve as comments on the reality of the shoddy film with which Lesley is involved.

The time scale in this play breaks with the straightforward chronology established in the other *Talking Heads*. Alan Bennett has chosen to begin his narrator's account about a week after the end of filming. Then, in a series of flashback scenes, we follow the sequence of events over what seems to be a rather hurried film-making in Lee-on-Solent until Lesley is home again. The final scene is set at dusk and Lesley is perhaps a little bit more thoughtful than usual, Although she seems to believe that she will 'have to live' with the fame that Gunther has ironically told her is coming her way, she is also recognising that she needs to acquire 'another skill', and at least one of her possibilities is related to the need to earn money.

In contrast, the first scene of the play, which takes place last of all, chronologically, is set in the morning, and Lesley is at her most horribly vivacious. She has digested her film experience and turned it into what she no doubt considers a riveting story that she will tell to anyone she can persuade to listen.

The sets go quite a long way towards telling the story in *Soldiering On*. By the fourth scene, Muriel's 'comfortable home' has become bare, stripped by the auctioneers, and in the last scene she is discovered in a 'plain boarding-house room', where her penurious state has forced her to take up residence. This sequence reinforces our understanding, from the second scene onwards, that Giles is likely to cause her financial downfall. Setting the last scene in the evening helps to set the mood for Muriel's acceptance that her previous life is over, and that the evening of her days is to be unfulfilled and lonely.

This monologue begins somewhere in East Anglia in April and ends 'out of season' in Hunstanton. As in *Bed Among the Lentils*, for the events of this play to be credible quite a lengthy time span is needed – probably about a year. The dramatic urgency of the story, however, has to be maintained and so the passage of time within the play is not emphasised and events seem to follow in fairly rapid succession.

The final play, like the first, has a somewhat claustrophobic atmosphere, underlined by the fact that the setting of all four scenes is Doris's home, to her a hygienic fortress against the dirt and confusion of the world. In the first three scenes Doris is hoping to attract attention and help from 'outside' after her accident; by the fourth scene she has realised that help from outside will lead to the old people's home she dreads, and she has decided that she will let nature take its course and die in her own home. The change of sets supports this sequence of Doris's thought in the play: by the third scene, still thinking of rescue, she has reached the front door – the nearest point to people and life 'outside' which she mistrusts. Her withdrawal to the sitting room reflects her defiant, or wilful, rejection of the life that society offers her.

In *A Cream Cracker Under the Settee* the action gives the impression of being virtually continuous, although some hours must pass from her fall in the morning to the darkness that signals approaching night and, of course, Doris's death.

We do not see what would have been Doris's undignified progress across the floor between scenes. Doris cannot move easily and, though they are not immobilised, neither do the rest of the *Talking Heads*; their fixed positions help to give these narrators something of their mesmerising quality.

These notes about Alan Bennett's use of time and settings obviously refer directly to dramatic productions of the plays. Even if these monologues have to be read as short stories, however, it is relevant to consider these matters: to read the stage directions about settings will help to widen the scope of the imagination, and it is as natural when reading a short story to take account of its time scale as it is when watching a play.

Themes

In these short plays the themes are usually those long associated with the human condition: loneliness and alienation, a failure to understand others, a lack of self-knowledge.

Alan Bennett's characters are very much of the end of the century: they are individuals at odds with contemporary society whose traditional structures – the Church, the family, neighbourliness – have changed, yet somehow these characters have found means of surviving.

Loneliness and alienation from a changed society

All the characters in these monologues are lonely or they are threatened with loneliness, and this loneliness stems from misreading the rules of a changed society. Miss Irene Ruddock, for example, is lost in a society that no longer has any firm boundaries or structure. In the past a neighbourly interest was welcomed, but no personal contact has ever been initiated by her with the young family she is spying on, nor by them with her. The Church which once offered order and security is debased: when the vicar offers to prove his identity by showing her his cross, she dismisses it by saying that a cross does not mean anything nowadays and anyone can wear it. It is no longer a potent symbol. Only in prison does she find an orderly structure to life.

Muriel faces loneliness through a breakdown in family values, first by gradually learning that her husband has sexually abused their daughter; secondly by being betrayed by her son, who should be protecting her rather than stealing from her.

Doris, entirely alone, looks back nostalgically to an ordered past when streets were clean and neighbours were friendly, and strangers did not urinate in your garden. The only alternative to her loneliness is being institutionalised.

Most of the plays make the audience conscious of the efforts of the various organisations of the welfare state to cope with the different needs of the narrators and the unseen characters. These efforts are seen as poor substitutes for support for the individual traditionally given by family, friends and neighbours, and are grudgingly or ungratefully received by the beneficiaries, as are the well-intentioned visits of the clergy. Loneliness is endemic amongst the *Talking Heads*, but visiting vicars are dealt with combatively by Miss Ruddock and Mrs Whittaker, and seen as unattractively human by Muriel Carpenter and, of course, Susan, the clergyman's wife.

Several characters suffer from mental illness: Graham, Miss Ruddock, Muriel Carpenter's daughter, who all have to take 'tablets'; this can, of course, represent medical progress or can seem in *Talking Heads* to show the health services's universal response to individual problems. Something like a cure, however, is achieved for Margaret, Muriel's daughter (ironically not in the comfortable private sector), and Graham is not negative about his doctor, Dr Chaudhury – although he uses the prescription of 'a stable environment' as emotional blackmail to try to stop his mother from marrying Frank Turnbull. Miss Ruddock, who triumphantly routs the vicar with her unexpected claim of atheism, is someone who never doubts her own judgment and she attacks the unfamiliar doctor and the manufacturers of her 'tablets' when she calls at the surgery. In the end, she flushes away her prescription down the lavatory. She accepts that she 'gets a bit upset' but clearly thinks that it is not medication she needs but support in her role as guardian of public morality. In the cases both of Graham and Miss Ruddock, when they have what they want from life they are not ill: Graham apparently manages well when he is assured of his mother's company; Miss Ruddock positively blooms when she is forcibly integrated into prison society. Muriel's daughter's case is different: her illness is caused by her father's abuse and when her father dies we assume that the secrecy and silence that have been a result of the betrayal can be broken. Her illness is not the rather vague malaise that affects Graham and Miss Ruddock, and which can be seen in *Talking Heads* as a metaphor for dissatisfaction with their lives.

Unhappiness

Muriel Carpenter says that she is not a 'tragic woman' and Miss Ruddock would not accept the magistrate's comment that she was 'more to be pitied than anything else'. It is perhaps part of their strategies for survival that the narrators do not see themselves as pitiable and if Alan Bennett's central theme is that the human condition is a tragi-comedy then their lack of self-knowledge contributes both to the tragedy and the comedy of the narrators. It also reminds us uncomfortably of the French poet Baudelaire's (1821–67) famous comment to his reader: '*Hypocrite lecteur! mon semblable, mon frère!*' (Hypocritical reader, my double, my brother!). These narrators live in a world which we share, and which we understand only too well.

Each of the narrators finds a different way in which to be unhappy. Graham's loneliness is assuaged only by the company of his mother and his pride maintained by his dominance of her thoughts and tastes – the world outside is too difficult for him, it seems, and his taste in pornography suggests, too, that he might have difficulty in coming to terms with his sexuality. Nevertheless, whilst he is secure at home and can keep alive his mother's interest in him, he survives and enjoys sharing his views on current affairs and his outings with Mrs Whittaker. Bennett makes us feel perhaps that tragedy looms, however: Mrs Whittaker is old and frail and soon he will be alone.

Susan's unhappiness is harder to analyse. The dramatist has created a witty, complex narrator who is not so helpless that she could not have avoided a loveless marriage and a role which ties her to the Church in which she has lost faith. Her disappointment seems to relate to her whole world and drink is her means of escape. When she finds herself almost by chance in an exotic affair, we see that she needs a lover rather than a husband shared by all the parish. For a while she finds Ramesh's unfamiliar view of life refreshing, but he is able to move on and she is not. She survives by mocking not only the fatuities of her life but herself, as well. She 'seems a different woman' in the last scene but we probably have little confidence in any future happiness. Bennett's narrator is a subversive, not one of society's more comfortable members.

Miss Ruddock's story does have a happy ending. When she is brought face to face with some of life's more brutal realities in prison she is able to exchange her extreme loneliness for participation in the excitement of learning and the fascination of being part of the prison community and actually being able to offer sympathy and help. Like Doris, in *A Cream Cracker Under the Settee* she feels painfully at the beginning of the monologue that neighbours are not what they used to be, that there are too many changes in her street and that the world beyond her front door is unknown and dangerous. It is very much worse for some people, she discovers in prison, than she could ever have imagined, and Alan Bennett uses this discovery as her means of redemption.

Lack of self-knowledge

Poor Lesley in *Her Big Chance* lacks self-knowledge to a degree almost beyond redemption. Alan Bennett's theme of loneliness is present here, too, and all the more poignant for Lesley's failure to recognise what a lonely woman she is. Resolutely bright and cheerful, apparently dedicated to self-improvement and professionalism, she seems to believe that she is doing everything right when really she is unable even to communicate on a human level – except in bed, perhaps. Alan Bennett shows her to be an artificial product of her belief that there are rules to be learned about human behaviour and that they can be found in pseudo-psychological handbooks. In failing to respond to other people naturally but trying to manipulate them to her advantage, as advised by her superficial reading, she in fact becomes easy prey to the manipulations of others. Alan Bennett has dealt savagely with this narrator, perhaps as a revenge for his past suffering at auditions with actors and actresses, of whom he says he has 'met dozens' like Lesley.

Muriel Carpenter is another character who lacks self-awareness and is sometimes seriously unable to understand what is going on. She prides herself on surviving – 'soldiering on' – and at the end of the monologue challenges loneliness with her radio and television. She also challenges our view of her as a tragic woman, although there is more of tragedy than comedy in her decline, particularly since Alan Bennett lets us know that her own rose-spectacled view of her dreadful son is the cause of it.

Doris, like Miss Ruddock, resents what she sees as a decline in society's values and leads a lonely life amongst supposedly unfriendly neighbours. Alan Bennett gives Doris what is virtually a heroic role – something that certainly does not figure in any of the other narrators' roles – when she decides that she has a choice between the old people's home and death. To choose death is an epic decision, even though it is taken by a woman of little significance in society, and the resolution of this play is sad but satisfying, given Doris's view of her prospects.

The 'little' person in society

If the main themes of Alan Bennett's *Talking Heads* are loneliness and failure to understand life and oneself, he also pays respect to the right to attention of the 'little' person in society. Foolish, wilful, vain, mistaken as they might be, the narrators are given substance and demand a hearing. Their problems may be the problems of ordinary and often unfortunate people at a particular point in time, but there is a universality about their narratives that touches us and finds us confused between laughter and tears.

Style and language

If you have ever recorded a classroom or seminar discussion or a lively party conversation, you will know how, once out of context, the dialogue sounds incomplete, fragmented and much less interesting than you would have expected.

It is easy to recognise therefore that, whilst persuading us that we are listening to a monologue employing ordinary everyday speech, Alan Bennett nevertheless has had to bring much writer's skill to bear on his raw material. He obviously has a very good ear for the nuances of speech and many of the memorable phrases of his monologues probably owe their inclusion to a writer's notebook recording snatches of overheard conversations. His task has been to create convincingly naturalistic speech which carries the whole burden of character realisation and the telling of a story. In fact, each narrator tells two stories – an account of events as the speaker sees it, and the story that we are meant to understand through our own assessment of what has really been going on.

In each of the plays Alan Bennett makes us gradually realise that these are unreliable narrators – that we are meant to see beyond what they are saying and to understand the real story 'to the meaning of which they are not entirely privy', as he writes. In this way a collusion is invited between the dramatist and the viewer or reader and the means by which this is done demands skills far beyond what has been called 'drama from gossip'.

These general comments apply to all the *Talking Heads* plays and it is this approach – the apparently realistic speech, and the transparency of the narrator – which links them stylistically. Each narrator is however memorably distinct as is the story told.

Graham's is one of Alan Bennett's 'northern' voices, His view of life is a gloomy one, and this is highlighted by contrast with the merriment of his mother and Frank Turnbull. A repeated phrase by which we remember Graham is 'I didn't say anything' – expressing both his disapproval and also his inability to influence events. Graham is fussy, and very interested in domestic details, and his gloom and his fussiness come together in the title of the monologue, *A Chip in the Sugar*. This distasteful detail in the 'common' red café where Frank takes them can also be seen as a metaphor for vulgar Frank's interruption to what Graham sees as his pleasant existence with his mother.

The title of *Bed Among the Lentils* too is a literal description as well as carrying the suggestion that Susan needed an exotic or even bizarre escape from her predictable husband and his unpleasing embraces. Susan is full of questions which she does not actually voice: she would like to ask

Geoffrey whether he actually believes in God or whether he just does a job like any other, or whether he thinks that Jesus ever 'smirked'. She also questions her own failure to find fulfilment in life, where Alan Bennett uses something approaching stream of consciousness passages. ('Stream of consciousness' or 'interior monologue' are phrases used of a technique which attempts to describe the experience of the mind and the welter of thoughts and feelings that pass through it. It is not usually relevant in commenting on *Talking Heads* because the narrator's first purpose is to unfold a fairly brisk plot.)

Susan's monologue, unusually in *Talking Heads*, is full of ironic comments: for instance, when Geoffrey preaches a sermon concluding that the money put in the offertory plate is a symbol of offering to God everything in life including sex, Susan comments 'I could only find 10p'. Susan is perfectly aware of the irony in this remark, and we share the humour with the character in this particular monologue, rather than, as in the others, with the dramatist.

With Miss Ruddock we are back with what might seem a particularly northern relish for the supposedly correct approach to the minutiae of everyday life. She is aggressive and has a scathing word or two for nearly everyone and everything. Her narrative is brisk and she has a strident social confidence which makes her one or two solecisms more amusing: for instance, she congratulates herself on taking up smoking, since she feels it will be useful if she ever has to be involved in toasting the Queen. Alan Bennett seems to imbue her fountain pen, the 'trusty Platignum', with a symbolic quality. It is the cause of both her downfall and her prospect of a new life and to Miss Ruddock it is a reminder of her mother, who bought it for her on one of her last outings before she died. Her mother and the memories of a happier past, a lost golden age, are linked with the pen. Although the pen is implicated in the slanderous letters written by Miss Ruddock, it is included in her redemption, since in prison she puts her letter-writing skills to a more sympathetic use.

The would-be sophisticated Lesley in *Her Big Chance* is presented as unrelentingly pretentious and tedious, and Alan Bennett swamps her speech with clichés, something that he limits in the other *Talking Heads* plays where the narrators, although apparently colloquial speakers, are given individual patterns of speech, and clichés are not the most important means of establishing character. Lesley's first two brief paragraphs, however, show the dependence of her monologue on cliché: 'look to the future'; 'under your belt'; 'line of duty'; 'takes in their stride'; 'tussle with my conscience'; 'things were never going to be the same again'; 'a woman at the crossroads' all appear. Her party conversation, too, with Spud, shows clichés as substitute for real communication: the last three lines on page 57 include 'stamping ground'; 'for my sins'; 'a far-ish cry'; 'I didn't fall off the Christmas tree yesterday'.

Some of the unseen characters are apparently as unperceptive as herself. Bennett gives Terry, the animal handler, a very feeble joke about mushroom growing. Lesley's reaction is unexpected although it pinpoints the dullness underlying her pert style: she sees the joke as unsuccessful not because of its familiarity and weakness but because it fails to take into account developments in the mushroom-growing trade. On the other hand, Nigel, the director's hard-pressed assistant, is given a trenchant style which contrasts tellingly with Lesley's elaborate but well-worn conversational style.

Muriel Carpenter's character and her circle are to some extent established by clichés which indicate the middle-class and an armed forces background. There are quite a few phrases associated with the military on the first two pages, for instance, of *Soldiering On*: 'coward's way out'; 'lived to fight another day'; 'staunch the flood'; 'back into the fray'; 'tackling the debris'. The other clichés which help to establish character are all well tried and, as Alan Bennett says of his narrators themselves, old-fashioned. Examples among many are 'bearded him in his den', 'a drop in the ocean' and 'orphans of the storm'. Alan Bennett gives Muriel other character-establishing tricks of speech. She uses the impersonal pronoun 'one' occasionally – for example, 'one would have fought tooth and nail to keep her in the private sector', and also often uses a brisk-sounding abbreviated narrative, suited to the style of an officer's or executive's wife. Look, for instance, at the paragraph on page 76, beginning 'Job sorting out . . .' which demonstrates Muriel's memo style communication, perhaps intended to conceal emotion, but in reality revealing it. The last page of her narrative, as she explains how she passes her time, contains a great many of these truncated sentences.

Alone among characters in the *Talking Heads* plays, Muriel laughs. Susan is witty, of course, but her humour is bitter. Muriel is able to laugh even at the funeral: when a mourner turns out to be an ex-prisoner who has attended the funeral out of respect for Ralph, Muriel says that she 'shrieked'. Later in the day, she and Mabel have 'a good laugh and a good cry' over the emotional effect on them of Ralph's wellington boots. She even makes a joke (page 73) about throwing herself into the canal, which is unrecognised by a receptionist who obviously does not expect humour from the recently widowed Muriel. She jokes, too, towards the end of the narrative about the possibility of reincarnation, which she says she just hopes will not be in Hunstanton, where she seems doomed to spend her sad final days. Her ability to accept her plight, even to laugh, is perhaps what enables her to say that she is not a 'tragic woman', and yet her cheerful stoicism certainly adds to the poignancy of her situation.

Doris has something in common with Mrs Whittaker – both are in their seventies and both can be quite truculent although Mrs Whittaker is still interested in enjoying herself, whereas Doris is a prisoner of her anxiety over the state of her house and garden. Alan Bennett has given Doris a lively and forceful style of speech, not unlike that of Mrs Whittaker, although Doris's narrative often betrays her lack of education: 'I never saw no list' or 'Them's her leaves', for example (page 83). She swears mildly: 'oh hell, the flaming buffet' when recounting the circumstances of her accident, but later uses the even less offensive 'Oh stink'. She uses very few clichés; when she does use the phrase 'on the carpet' it is with a double meaning as she sees the opportunity of an attack on Zulema, and her speech is very idiosyncratic – a mixture of the very direct and colloquial – for example, 'great lolloping lamp post-smelling articles' or 'graves, gardens, everything's to follow' – with some unexpectedly heavyweight words like 'surreptitious' or 'gregarious'. Doris also uses broken sentence structure quite often; unlike Muriel's brisk speech, hers often suggests something like stream of consciousness, especially as her thoughts wander more and more to the past.

The choice of names for the narrators is significant, and especially so in the case of Doris and her husband Wilfred. As she says, they are names from the past, the names of people who do not belong any more. Zulema, on the other hand, has a name which comes from a culture that Doris is not familiar with. In this play, Zulema represents authority and the present whereas Doris knows she and the world she remembers are finished.

The wedding photograph of Doris and Wilfred is a strong symbol: it has fallen from the wall as a result of Doris's endless quest for dust and the glass has cracked. This probably represents the destructive nature of Doris's cleaning mania, the loss of Wilfred 'tidied into the grave' as Alan Bennett writes, and particularly, with Doris's impending death, the end of the marriage as it had continued to exist in Doris's memory.

We can see, looking at the plays both individually and as a linked group, that Alan Bennett has marshalled many different possibilities to serve his purpose in creating credible characters and stories. The convincing style of speech he has given to each narrator represents probably the most compelling means of giving them life. He also uses parallels in the stories and symbolism to underline his themes. Perhaps the aspect of style and language most peculiarly his is his unerring identification of the details of everyday life that tell us so much about a person. This can refer to domestic details, to clothes – often mentioned – and even to food, which features in each monologue. The menu quoted by Graham in the 'common' red café; Susan's unappetising lunch for the bishop; Miss Ruddock's hair-infested sausages; Lesley's fork lunch or finger buffet; Muriel's funeral feast and final boiled egg; Doris's frugal cream cracker – each of these apparently trivial references helps to pinpoint the character of the narrator or the situation. Even Alan Bennett's references to places that he identifies specifically are illuminating: Scarborough and Tenerife; Spain and Lee-on-Solent; Siena and Hunstanton – these pairs of places mentioned in three of the monologues show the tastes of the characters as well as the realities of the stories. The attention to detail, the examination of the minutiae of quotidian life, often supplies the clues which enable us to see his narrators in the round. What his narrators talk about is, after all, as necessary to our understanding as how they speak.

Part 4

Hints for study

Reading the texts

These short plays do not take long to read and you will need to go through each several times: you will be surprised how much more you find to interest you at each reading. You will have to decide how to tackle a group of short texts, which present advantages and disadvantages over a long, continuous work. Probably it will be best to read all the plays at first; this will give you a feeling of what links the monologues in terms of themes and style. Then you will need to set to work with your notebook to study each play in turn.

First, you must examine what the narrator tells us in each monologue and whether or not it actually happens; you can do this by making your own summary. The summaries given in these *Notes* will help, but you need to be clear in your own mind as to the events described. This will be quite straightforward. Then you will have to use your imagination, as Alan Bennett suggests in the 'Introduction', the way you would if you were reading a short story; each of these narrators tells a one-sided story and you have to see how Bennett has made it possible for us to make judgments about characters and situations which result in a rather different reading of each monologue. The individual commentaries given offer some hints as to what assessments we might make but, again, you need to make up your own mind as to what is significant in establishing a more rounded view of the story.

This is where you should start to make detailed notes. The narrators innocently drop clues which guide us to a fuller understanding: we are alerted to Susan's drinking, for instance, by the early reference to the off-licence woman's lack of a smile; to Giles's dishonesty by the over-lavish lunch he buys his mother; or to Simon's astonishment at Lesley's pretentiousness by his overheard phone call. You will also need to make a note of ambiguities or meanings hidden from the narrator in the reported speech that figures so frequently in the monologues. Tricks of speech, repetitions, reference to revealing memories of the past will all be helpful and should be noted with their page numbers so that you can easily find them again. This is the material with which you will be able to support your own interpretation of the story; if you cannot find these supportive details it may well be that what you want to say cannot be justified and you will need to re-think your interpretation of the play.

At some point in your study of the texts, probably when you have already formulated some ideas about them, it would be ideal to see a video or listen to an audio-tape of the original productions in which Alan Bennett was involved, directing one himself. The acting was polished and professional and the subtleties of the plays were very fully revealed. However, it may well be that this will not be possible. Whether or not you have been able to enjoy a professional performance, do try reading the text aloud yourself; if you are able to work with other students, try various approaches which bring out both the comedy and tragedy, paying particular attention to timing, and discuss what it is that leads to a good reading. If you are working alone, it is even more helpful to read the text aloud. Even though the monologues have many of the qualities of the short story, the skilful speech clamours to be spoken aloud.

Preparing for an examination

There are many particular skills which have to be brought into play in order to write successful English literature examination essays. The first essential is to know your text – or texts in the case of *Talking Heads*. Some examination boards allow you to take your set books into the examination with you; this offers an opportunity to enhance your essays and is certainly not intended to undermine the need for thorough familiarity with the text. In any case you will have no time to spare for vague searchings for half-remembered references in the text.

Knowing your texts is the key to being able to support the ideas you have already formulated about the plays, as has been mentioned above in 'Reading the texts'. Next you will need to assess what kind of question is likely to be asked about these monologues. Some suggested questions are set out below and you will see that they are likely to fall into different categories: if there are two possible questions on an examination paper, very likely one will be general and require you to refer to all or several of the plays, while a second may ask you to respond with reference to one or maybe two plays only. The more general questions may require you to comment on all or several of the plays in relation to genre, style, structure and themes; a question requiring you to give a closely detailed answer on one play only may require comment on all or any of the aspects already mentioned, but is also likely to ask for comment on characterisation and plot structure.

Look at the specimen questions and assess your ability to answer them. You will see that usually what is involved is an analysis of the ways in which Alan Bennett has made his work effective and here it is worth mentioning a familiar pitfall which you will need to avoid. If you were answering, for instance, question 5, about *Soldiering On*, you must remember that you are writing about a fictional character, brought to life only on the page by the skills of Alan Bennett, and not a living person. You must be careful not to respond by commenting on what this character should or should not have done and giving advice for the future, as though you were dealing with a case history or the difficulties of a real person. Although we would respond with laughter and sadness to Muriel's plight, literary criticism usually requires an analysis of the means by which the writer has evoked these feelings – that is to say you will need to write about not only *what* the writer has done, but *how* he has done it.

In your preliminary studies of these plays you should spend as long as is necessary on sorting out your ideas and the more written material you prepare the more helpful it will be to you later. Record this material in the form which you find most useful – notes, essays, key points on cards all have their place. As the time of the examination begins to draw near you will need to practise examination skills by writing timed essays. This pressure should help to test the clarity of your ideas and of course it is highly necessary to go into your examination with your views and supporting material already prepared: the examination room is no place to begin making up your mind about your response to the texts.

Choose the question to which you can offer the best answer – check this by making a brief plan if necessary – after deciding upon the scope of the question. You need to ask yourself what the examiner is going to be looking for in a good answer and thus make sure that what you include is relevant. Bear in mind that few if any English Literature questions these days are set to trick you – the aim is usually to give you a chance to show what you can do. Most questions will lend themselves to the possibility of a variety of answers, but relevance matters and needs to be considered before, during and on checking your answer. It is often a good idea to outline what you propose to cover in your introduction and to draw together your ideas at the end of your essay. Make your points clearly, illustrating them wherever appropriate with supporting evidence from the texts; if you use quotations, make them brief and telling.

In your written answer, let your individual response come through in the style of your essay; write naturally, but remember that slang and collo- quialisms are inappropriate (unless they are quotations from the writer) although they may make a point if used ironically between inverted commas. A second pitfall, related to the first mentioned above and also to be avoided, concerns *Talking Heads* in particular. The difficulties encoun- tered by the narrators (loneliness, mental illness, lack of self-knowledge or misunderstanding of others, for instance) are situations referred to frequently in the media – for example, in television serials and in articles in the press. The jargon often employed to discuss sociological problems should be avoided in your essay; as Alan Bennett says in his 'Introduc- tion', he has nothing against practical social work, but he quarrels with 'the jargon in which it's sometimes conducted'. So avoid the slick familiar phrases and you will demonstrate your understanding of a central point which the writer is making.

Specimen questions

1. In *A Chip in the Sugar* for whom do you find you have the most sympathy, Graham or Mrs Whittaker, and on what do you base your judgment?
2. In *Bed Among the Lentils* why do you think Ramesh rather than Geoffrey is able to persuade Susan to tackle her alcoholism?
3. How credible do you find the transformation in prison of Miss Ruddock in *A Lady of Letters*?
4. What means does Alan Bennett employ in *Her Big Chance* to let us understand the truth about Lesley?
5. 'I'm not a tragic woman,' says Muriel in *Soldiering On*. Do you agree?
6. What do you see as the significance of the photograph in its broken frame in *A Cream Cracker Under the Settee*?
7. Do you find tragedy or comedy more dominant in these plays?
8. Are the constraints of the monologue a strength or a weakness in *Talking Heads*?
9. The 'unseen' characters are important in these plays. Discuss how Alan Bennett presents two of these (for example, Mrs Whittaker, Geoffrey, Ramesh, Spud, Giles, Wilfred, Zulema).
10. Do the narrators represent ordinary people with purely contemporary problems, or do you find an element of timelessness in their situations? Discuss with reference to two or three of the plays.
11. What do you think is lost or gained by reading these plays as short stories rather than seeing performances on television or the stage?
12. John Wells has said that Alan Bennett employs 'the poetry of ordinary people's speech'. Discuss the style of these plays in relation to this comment.

Specimen answer

2. In *Bed Among the Lentils* why do you think Ramesh rather than Geoffrey is able to persuade Susan to tackle her alcoholism?

Susan finds her role as vicar's wife disappointing and unsatisfying; her fortuitous relationship with Ramesh is exciting and interesting in more ways than one, so it is not surprising that he is able to influence her.

Alan Bennett has created a wilful and subversive character in Susan, who is unlike the other narrators in *Talking Heads* in her degree of self-awareness. It may be somewhat puzzling that such a witty and critical woman has found herself married to a man whom she neither loves nor respects. She has also apparently failed to assess what would be expected of the wife of a clergyman. We are left in no doubt that her disaffection runs deep. She despises Geoffrey's perceived insincerity, watching what she sees as his 'performances' for the parishioners by making use of 'his schoolboy good looks', for instance, with cynical interest. She describes their love-making as 'rare and desiccated conjunctions' and takes care to avoid Geoffrey's amorous advances after a successful Sunday sermon. She observes her husband's ambitions for his career with amused detachment and fully recognises the final irony of the play in the fact that his anticipated promotion will owe much to her widely publicised alcoholism and Geoffrey's supposed support.

Susan's agnosticism makes her highly critical of the Church to which she is presumed to owe allegiance. She refers to Jesus familiarly, comparing him unfavourably even with Geoffrey, thinks he is no 'fun' and wonders if he ever 'smirked'. God, too, is dismissed as 'Geoffrey's chum' and, finally, as having 'no taste at all'. Nevertheless, her life revolves around the Church calendar and the daily parish duties. The dramatist shows us how deeply she is imbued with Church life and rituals by allowing her narrative to be interspersed with snatches – usually irreverent – of the Anglican prayers with which she is so familiar.

Alan Bennett starts to drop clues early in Susan's narrative about her drinking and we can see that she finds life desperately dull and her role particularly dispiriting. Her accounts of disasters caused by her drinking are very funny: the spilt milk when the Bishop comes to lunch, for instance, or the flower-arranging episode, or the missing communion wine for which cough mixture has to be substituted. Nevertheless, we cannot laugh too much, because these incidents are described by a lonely woman, who has no one in whom to confide and who is trying to find release through alcohol from the wretchedness of her existence.

'The beautiful Mr Ramesh, with wonderful legs' could hardly be more different from Geoffrey. He is a skilful, adventurous and enthusiastic lover, whose religion far from inhibiting his enjoyment accepts this as perfectly natural. He is a grocer, whose young wife is still in India, and we accept, although Susan does not say so, that he is an opportunist in their unlikely relationship. For her, it is a magical, guilt-free, exotic experience; she relishes Ramesh's courtship antics, and the lentils on which their bed is made up emphasise the strangeness of the situation. And not only is Susan free from any feeling of guilt with the natural Ramesh, she can take a private delight in the knowledge that neither Geoffrey nor anyone in her parish could guess where she was or what she was doing. She takes a wicked pleasure in drawing parallels between the dates of her exciting encounters with Ramesh and the Anglican Church festivals which for her were dull routine.

Not only are their sexual adventures enjoyable to Susan, but also the straightforward way in which Ramesh is able to talk about Hinduism contrasts with Susan's inability to discuss her religious doubts with Geoffrey. Alan Bennett begins and ends the play with Susan's comments about Jesus and God, which, subversive as they are, seem to focus the narrative on her agnostic inability either to believe or to become free of religion. And, at a key point if the story, she describes Ramesh in his spotless white shirt and loincloth as 'Like Jesus. Only not'. This seems to sum up Susan's attitude to sex and religion: Geoffrey and what she sees as 'his' religion to her mean insincerity and inhibitions, whereas Ramesh and Hinduism mean freedom from guilt, and naturalness. It is easy to see why Ramesh, for whose way of life Susan feels respect, is better able to influence her to tackle her alcoholism, than her husband.

Alan Bennett's last scene leaves us in doubt, of course, as to whether Susan's reformation is likely to last. The secret and private relationship she has enjoyed with Ramesh is over: he has been able to 'take the profit and move on', something which Susan admires but sounds unlikely to be able to emulate. She is back not quite in her old role, but still sharing a husband with the parish at large, and scornful, if amused, by the way in which her private problems have been the means of advancing Geoffrey's prospects.

Part 5

Suggestions for further reading

The text

ALAN BENNETT: *Talking Heads*, with an introduction by the dramatist, BBC Books, London, 1988.
Audio tape available from BBC Education, London.
Videos available from Focal Point Audio Visual, Portsmouth.

Other works by Alan Bennett

Objects of Affection and Other Plays for Television, BBC Publications, London, 1982.
The Writer in Disguise – five plays, Faber and Faber, 1985.
Writing Home, Faber and Faber, London, 1994.

Criticism

BRANDT, GEORGE W. (ED.): *British Television Drama in the 1980s*, Cambridge University Press, Cambridge, 1993: includes an essay on *Bed Among the Lentils* by Albert Hunt.

The author of these notes

Delia Dick was one of the first graduates of the Open University and was a post-graduate student at the University of Warwick. She has taught English Literature at various levels – in schools, in Further Education and in Higher Education. At present she lectures in twentieth-century literature at the University of Warwick and at Coventry University.